TERESA
OF
CALCUTTA

"It was in 1946 that she applied for permission to go out and work among the poor in the slums of the city. She felt this to be a fresh vocation, a vocation within a vocation, as she herself has expressed it.

GONXHA BOJAXHIU

She had had a glimpse of the poverty and squalor of the slums, of sick people who remained untended, of lonely men and women lying down to die on the pavement, of the thousands of orphaned children wandering around with no one to care for them.

It was among these people that she felt a call to work, and to spend the rest of her life, in daily contact with them. She left the sheltered world of the convent and the fashionable girls' school behind her. In 1948 she received permission to change from the uniform of the Loreto order to the customary cheap Indian sari...."

Professor John Sanness, Chairman, Norwegian Nobel Prize Committee, in Oslo, December 1979

ROBERT SERROU

TERESA OF CALCUTTA

A PICTORIAL BIOGRAPHY

WITH A FOREWORD BY

MALCOLM MUGGERIDGE

McGRAW-HILL BOOK COMPANY

NEW YORK   ST. LOUIS   SAN FRANCISCO

CONTENTS

A McGraw-Hill Co-Publication

Library of Congress Cataloging in
Publication Data.
Serrou, Robert.
    Teresa of Calcutta.
    1. Teresa, Mother, 1910–
    2. Nuns—India—Calcutta—
    Biography.
    3. Calcutta—Biography.
    I. Title.
BX 4406.5.Z8S47   266'.2'0924 [B]
80-18477
    ISBN 0-07-056319-5
    ISBN 0-07-056318-7 (pbk.)

Design by:
EMIL BÜHRER

Editor:
DAVID BAKER

Managing Editor:
FRANCINE PEETERS

Picture Procuration:
RUTH RÜEDI

Production Manager:
FRANZ GISLER

Printed by:
POLYGRAPHISCHE GESELLSCHAFT,
LAUPEN, SWITZERLAND

Bound by:
SCHUMACHER AG, SCHMITTEN

Composition by:
EDV+FILMSATZ AG, THUN

Photolithography by:
PESAVENTO AG, ZURICH

Printed in Switzerland

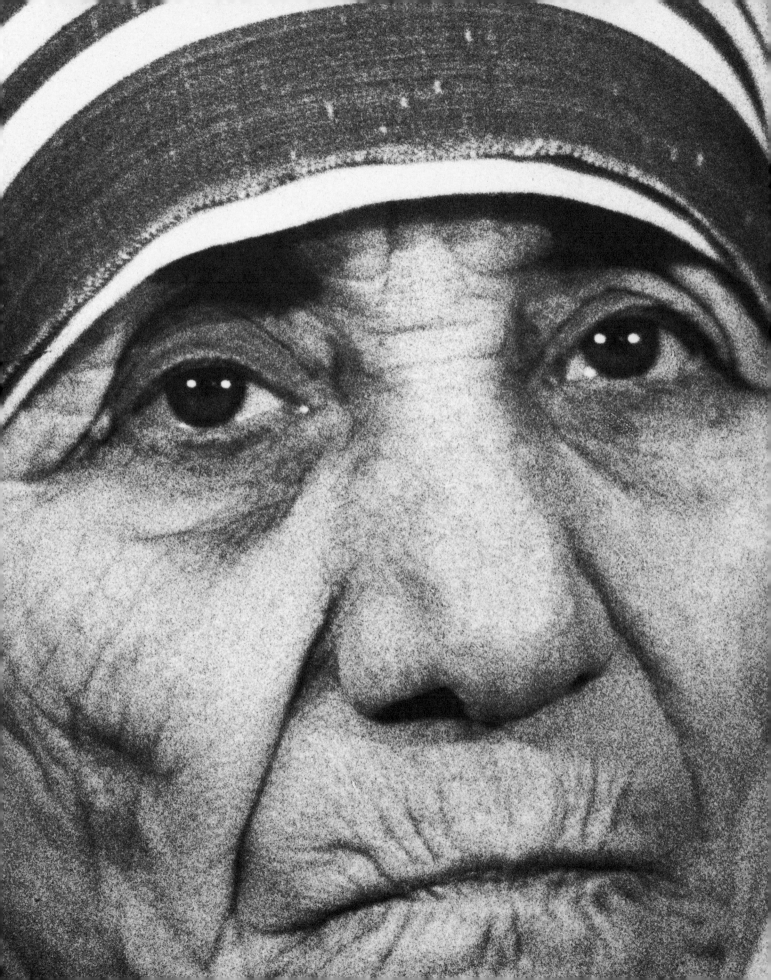

FOREWORD
BY MALCOLM MUGGERIDGE

It is now some thirty years since Mother Teresa, having first scrupulously obtained the permission of her ecclesiastical superiors, moved out from her Loreto convent in Calcutta and settled in the nearby slums. She embarked upon this heroic venture alone, with no money, precise plans, or, in worldly terms, resources of any kind. In her Christian faith, however, she had spiritual resources that were to prove inexhaustible in carrying love and compassion, not just to Calcutta's poor and outcast, but, directly or indirectly, to the poor and outcast everywhere. Plant love, St. John of the Cross tells us, and it will grow; Mother Teresa has demonstrated that this saying is as true in the twentieth century as it was in the sixteenth.

The order she in due course founded and continues to direct meticulously—the Missionaries of Charity—has come to have more than two hundred houses in different parts of the world, and new ones are being opened all the time. As an old journalist, it has fascinated me to note how, although—perhaps because!—she rarely opens a newspaper, and never listens to radio or watches television, she always knows exactly where the need for her Missionaries of Charity is greatest, and deploys them accordingly, with unerring accuracy. An international organization of co-workers has also been set up, and has spread far and wide. It is very characteristic of her that when someone suggested Friends of Mother Teresa as an appropriate name for such an organization, she remarked sharply that it was not so much friends as helpers that she wanted. So, Co-Workers of Mother Teresa it had to be. Also very characteristically, when it appeared that the co-workers were putting a disproportionate amount of effort into raising money for her work, she reminded them that their essential purpose was to comfort and help the lonely and afflicted, and that when money was needed it would surely come along—as, indeed, it always has.

Mundanely speaking, managing so large, widespread, and variegated an enterprise would require a whole skyscraper of executives with their attendant ancillary staff and computers; with typewriters tapping away, telephones ringing, tele-printers dispatching messages here, there, and everywhere; and an army of reps in dark suits and carrying briefcases, going, like Satan, to and fro' in the world and up and down in it. Needless to say, nothing of the kind is to be found in Mother Teresa's Calcutta headquarters in Lower Circular Road. There, the postulants are nowadays packed three, and sometimes four, in a room, so great is the pressure of girls all over the world eager to join the Missionaries of Charity. Their total possessions are two saris in the cheapest cloth obtainable and a bucket; they eat the same food as the poorest of the poor whom they serve; they have no fans, refrigeration, air-conditioning—none of the appurtenances considered as constituting quality of life. Yet I swear I have never experienced so sharp a sense of the joy of belonging to God's creation, and of the love which pervades it, as when I have been among them.

How is it that in this secular age someone like Mother Teresa should have become one of the most widely known and best-loved women of her time despite her unfashionable piety and orthodoxy? How does it come about that, just when the religious orders everywhere are losing their appeal and falling into disarray, hers, with a rule that even St. Theresa of Avila might have considered severe, goes on growing and flourishing? Certainly, she has no exceptional gifts of eloquence or charisma as these are currently appreciated; her invariable and utterly sincere response to the distinctions and honors—such as the lately awarded Nobel Peace Prize—that come her way, is: "I am not worthy." It might, indeed, be said that her ordinariness is itself a kind of rare beauty, as her homilies, addressed without adaptation to any and every kind of audience, ranging between lepers in her charge and sophisticated cardinals and dons, are, in their simplicity and sincerity, a kind of rare eloquence.

Recently, I had the honor of introducing her—actually, of course, no introduction was needed—at a service in the Cambridge University Church after she had received an honorary degree. From where I was sitting, I could see the rapt, attentive faces of the huge congregation that had come to hear her. She used no notes, and never once raised her voice. Yet every word was clear and audible as she spoke of her special vocation to love and serve derelicts left to die in the streets of Calcutta, babies thrown away in dust-bins, all those whom the world rejected and despised everywhere. However, it is not just in her words and her works that her appeal lies, nor in the beauty of holiness that her presence conveys, nor even in her loving care of the afflicted, whether in mind or body or soul, seeing in each and every one of them, irrespective of circumstances, Christ Himself. There is something else—some special luminosity, which, as we discovered when we were making a television program, *Something Beautiful For God*, about her and her work, even registers itself on film.

This luminosity, I am convinced, is the outward and visible manifestation of the inward and invisible love which lies at the heart of our mortal existence; for those who have eyes to see, shining triumphantly through the misery and darkness we create, with our wills in the pursuit of power, with our bodies in the pursuit of carnality, and with our egos in the pursuit of self-gratification. A Mother Teresa comes into the world, as the Savior she serves so faithfully and ardently did, to keep the light shining in a dark and confused time. God has sent her, as through history he sends His special messengers. Let us, then, be thankful for so great a mercy, and, in our thankfulness, honor, love, and help her.

© MALCOLM MUGGERIDGE, 1980

For Teresa there is no difference between the poorest of the poor and the richest of the rich. Even when a king awards her the world's greatest honor—in this case the Nobel Prize—it has no more worth for her than the outstretched hand of a beggar. This handshake from the king of Norway to this old woman dressed in her sari is an acknowledgement from the rich of all those millions of people in the world who lack the bare necessities of life—who do not even have a stone on which to lay their heads. Teresa is a living reproach, a call to order.
A king's hand is smooth and manicured, perfumed and like a bright new object. A poor person's hand is ravaged, callused, and bony. We might speculate which of the two Teresa would prefer. The writer Georges Bernanos, perhaps better than anyone, understood this viewpoint when he wrote in Humble Children *these words that could have been written by Teresa herself: "I am no enemy to extreme wealth, because it is a burden which weighs almost as heavily as a great name... I say that the world will be saved by the Poor.... The modern world has no time to hope, to love, or to dream. Rather it is the poor who hope...." Teresa has embraced the vocation of poverty most intensely, fanatically. Her hand extended to the king is, finally, a lesson in humility, a symbol that fortune prevents no man from being, in the eyes of God, a simple poor person. Her hand extended to a lost soul signifies that she identifies entirely with him. For God the rich and the poor man have the same worth, the same dignity.*

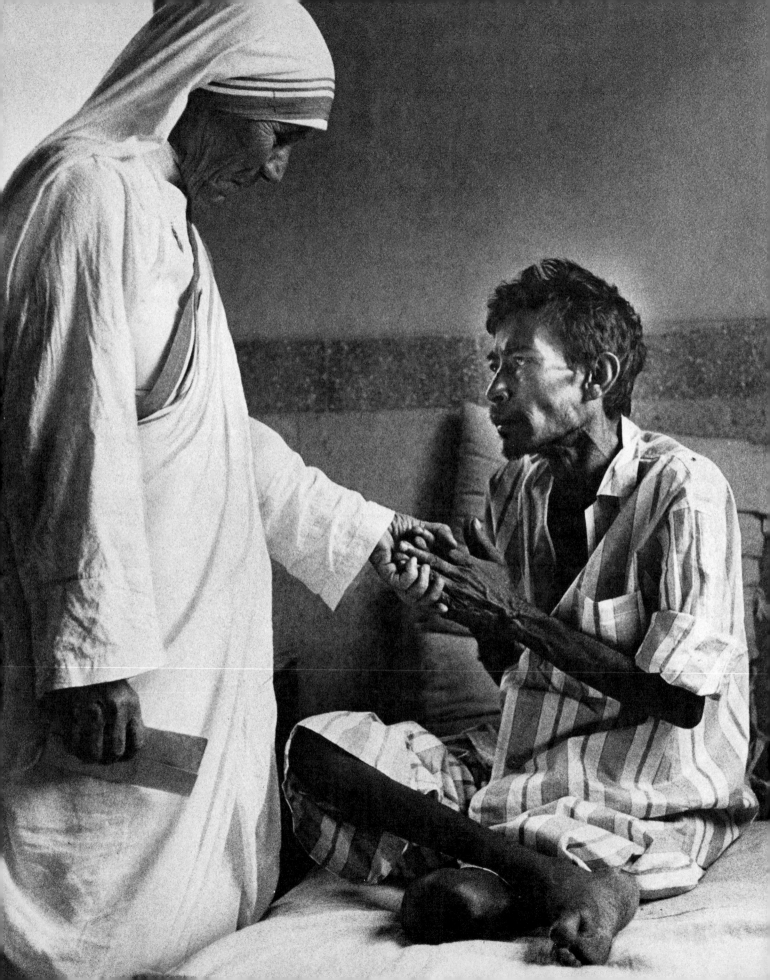

"A DROP OF DELIVERANCE
IN AN OCEAN OF SUFFERING"

A modest little countrywoman standing in the gilded splendor of a Norwegian palace: it might have been a scene from a fairytale. But in Oslo, on 10 December 1979, the fairytale came true. Dressed in a simple white sari edged in blue, with a cross on her left shoulder, this woman—her face furrowed, parched, almost mummified as if congealed by thirty years of apocalyptic horrors—was about to receive the world's greatest honor, the Nobel Peace Prize. She is Mother Teresa of Calcutta.

Who is Mother Teresa? One of those inspired fanatics of the same breed as the great Apostles or the mystics. In a word, a saint. A saint who has taken on not only all of the misery of the world, but something even greater, its poor. Never was a Nobel Peace Prize more deserved. The Norwegians themselves, who had become increasingly indifferent about the coveted prize, felt a resurgence of interest when they heard about Mother Teresa. No doubt as she sat in the DC 9 Cunnard Viking which brought her from Rome to Oslo, she wasn't anticipating the triumphal welcome this Protestant country was preparing for her. Nor did it matter to her.
Seated next to two of the original Indian sisters of the congregation, she spent the trip praying and going over her acceptance speech, eating nothing except an occasional nibble of bread, a tomato slice, a bit of lettuce. When she disembarked in the frozen nordic capital at minus 10 °C (14 °F), some thousand people stood waiting for her, candles in hand.
Apparently she had been forgiven for having canceled the Nobel banquet, which according to a sacred tradition is held at the Hotel Continental each year on this occasion. The more than six thousand dollars thus saved would be added to the $ 190,000 prize money and the innumerable other little sums that had been collected throughout Norway.

Among these sums, the one that must have moved her most profoundly was the offering handed her by a little girl at a reception held in the hall of a Lutheran parish: $ 175 donated by children out of their own pocket money. Overwhelmed, Mother Teresa mounted the platform and grasping the microphone declared, "Yes, money is necessary. But to increase its value, we must season it with love. Then, like a boomerang, love returns to its source." Then, tireless despite her sixty-nine years, she took her leave of the audience, bowing as she always does in the typical Indian manner—her hands joined as if in prayer, to express her gratitude.
The awarding of the Nobel Peace Prize to Mother Teresa seemed to make everyone happy. It was a choice that promised to restore some of the prestige that the Nobel Prize had lost in recent years. For in fact, many persons both in Norway and elsewhere, no matter what their political views, had become skeptical of late about the prize. To many the whole thing had become a farce ever since Kissinger and Le Duc Tho were awarded the world's most prestigious honor in 1973. (Sadat and Begin were less controversial.) Elected for a six-year term, which is only renewable once, the five-member committee is entrusted to nominate the winner or winners (since there can be two). This committee meets in a mansion in Oslo, in a silk-lined hall decorated with the portraits of all the Nobel laureates since the prize was created in 1901. A half-dozen times, from February to October, they sit at a mahogany table and process all of the candidates—around fifty each year.
It is a little-known fact that in 1938, just after the Munich Agreement, the names of Hitler and Chamberlain were proposed, and so was that of Mussolini, who had just invaded Ethiopia.
The subject of Alfred Nobel himself has not escaped controversy. Everyone knows him as the creator of the prize that bears his name, but he is primarily the inventor of dynamite and the owner of 350 patents—most notably for a smokeless gunpowder and a kind of silk. It is forgotten that he stipulated in a first will that the wealth from his inventions be used for the construction of crematoriums in several cities. It was only the ban on cremation by the Vatican (since rescinded) that forced him to change his last wishes and to decide on creating the Nobel Prize. "I did a lot for peace," he used to say, referring to his work with gunpowder, "because when nations have a means of such destruction at their disposal, they can just dismiss their armies." Nobel knew whereof he spoke.

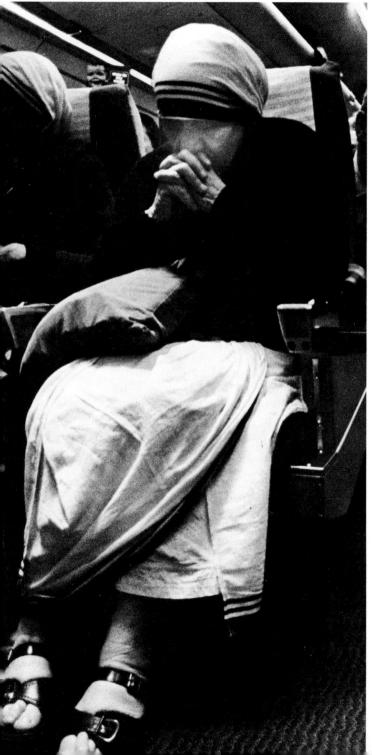

The first to receive his prize in 1901 was Henri Dunant, the founder of the Red Cross. Among the most famous recipients have been Albert Schweitzer in 1952, Martin Luther King in 1964, and organizations such as the Red Cross and (in 1977) Amnesty International. Of course scientists, chemists, biologists, doctors, and writers have also been awarded, not the Nobel Prize for Peace, but a prize in their specialty. Since its creation, there have been 112 physicians, 91 chemists, 75 writers, and 74 Nobel Peace Prizes, including Mother Teresa. Today we know that the Prize jury hesitated to bestow the prize on her because she faced a formidable adversary, namely Monsignor Oscar Romero, bishop of San Salvador, who was

assassinated on 25 March 1980 while he was celebrating the mass.

The Nobel Prize is "a drop of deliverance in an ocean of suffering," she said on learning of the decision of the Norwegian Parliament. Yes, only a drop of water, but added to others it can become a mighty river....

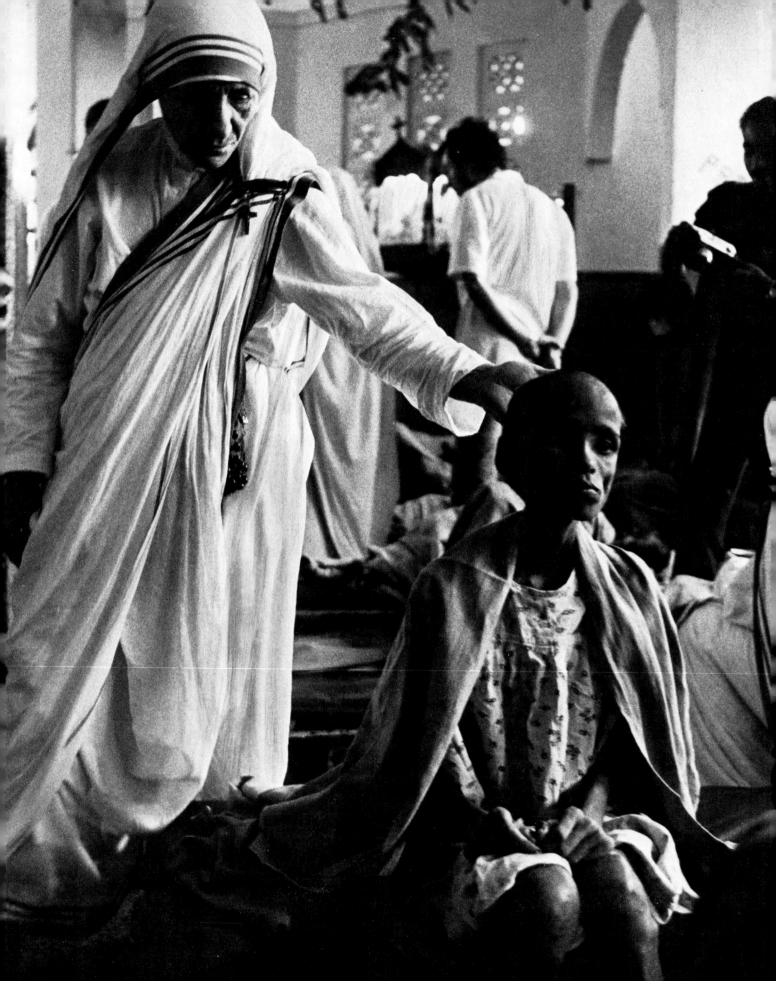

TERESA AND ST. FRANCIS

Let there be no pride or vanity in the work.
The work is God's work, the poor are God's poor.
Put yourself completely under the influence
of Jesus, so that he may think his thoughts
in your mind, do his work through your hands,
for you will be all-powerful
with him who strengthens you.

MOTHER TERESA

Lord, make me an instrument of Your peace,
Where there is hatred, let me sow love;
Where there is injury, pardon;
Where there is doubt, faith;
Where there is despair, hope;
Where there is darkness, light;
And where there is sadness, joy.
O divine Master, grant that I may not
So much seek to be consoled as to console;
To be understood as to understand;
To be loved as to love;
For it is in giving that we receive;
It is in pardoning that we are pardoned;
And it is in dying
That we are born to eternal life.

AMEN

This prayer written seven centuries ago by St. Francis of Assisi has become so closely associated with Mother Teresa that she could almost be considered its author. She has incorporated these words into the official daily prayer of the Missionaries of Charity, and she spoke St. Francis' prayer at the beginning of her Nobel Prize acceptance speech.

In many ways, Sister Teresa has fashioned her entire life work according to the spirit of *Il Poverello* ("The Little Pauper"). The two personalities have a good deal in common. Francis, son of a knight, enjoyed a charmed youth; Teresa also had a happy, comfortable childhood. Both had been suddenly seized with the same devotion to God and to the poor. No doubt, seven hundred years ago she would have followed him just like the rich young noblewoman Clare, who with her own disciples founded one of the most important of the Fran-

ciscan orders. Clare was a zealot of God, like Francis, like Teresa. It is certainly not insignificant that one day Francis wrote a kind of encomium to religious zeal: "Oh, Christ, you have ravished my heart, and yet you tell me that I must be moderate in order to love. But you did not restrain yourself high on the cross, when you embraced all mankind with such rapture." These words too could have been uttered by Teresa herself, for her love is expressed through prayer. To prayer she added action. How can you stand by the destitute, she thought, if you don't spend all your energies ceaselessly ferreting out the neglected and innocent.

Francis of Assisi placed poverty above all else. For poverty he renounced everything that can make life seem attractive, and thus he was able to bear witness for the poor. Teresa followed in his footsteps.

SOMEWHERE IN YUGOSLAVIA

In Skopje in Yugoslavia . . . . I lived at home and with my parents; we children used to go to a non-Catholic school but we also had very good priests who were helping the boys and the girls to follow their vocation according to the call of God. It was then that I first knew I had a vocation to the poor.

To bear witness, to consecrate one's life to the poorest, to seek them out wherever they are, to learn from them, listen to them, understand them—these are things which cannot be contrived or improvised. An existence devoted to the exercise of charity is an inherited privilege. It is a gift that is received somehow, sometime during childhood or adolescence, before one is even aware of the calling. For all saints whoever they are—and not just monks and nuns, for many secular saints have accomplished miracles simply for the sake of human dignity, without claiming the mission for God—for all of them, this need has been revealed through the childhood subconscious, at their mothers' knees, by the example of their families, through contact with the earth, with a fatherland and its history.

14

THE YEAR 1910

Mother Teresa never concealed the fact that between twelve and eighteen years she had never dreamed of becoming a nun. Only at eighteen did she decide to leave everything, and from then on she never once doubted her decision. It is impossible to understand or to get to know this woman, who is a Yugoslavian of Albanian descent, without seeing her in the context of her origins, her historical environment. In order for us really to grasp her, we must make a pilgrimage to Slavic land. This we must do if only to imagine, with a minimum risk of confusion, what she learned from her ancestors. In short, we must return to the roots.

She was born Gonxha (i.e., Agnes) Bojaxhiu on 27 August 1910 at Skopje, in a part of Macedonia that became Yugosla-

At the time of Teresa's birth, Turkey still ruled the land called Macedonia, as it had since the fourteenth century. Sultan Mohammed Reshad V (in power 1909–1918) visited her native city of Skopje, amid much pomp, in 1911—just two years before Macedonia was freed from the Turkish overlords.

vian territory after World War II. Her family, which originally included five children although only Gonxha and two others survived, was originally of peasant stock. Her father, Nikola Bojaxhiu, became a contractor with a successful construction business. He and her mother, Dronda, settled in Skopje shortly after the turn of the century.

Gonxha's family were Albanians, not Macedonians, and thus they had a particularly unstable status in this far from stable land.

In 1910, the year of her birth, Skopje (known as Uskup to the Turks) was a city of some 20,000 persons (5 percent of its present population), still under Turkish domination, though their rule was to end in the Balkan Wars of 1912–1913. In 1911, the town was refurbished and decorated for the official visit of Sultan Mehmed Reshad V. The first tramway line had just been laid, the principal streets were being paved, and where the paving was not yet complete, the hosts spread the streets with oriental carpets for the Sultan's procession. The city was to change hands several times during the local and world wars, including a period of occupation by Albanian mountaineers whose seizure of Skopje helped lead to the proclamation of a free Albania in 1912. By the time Gonxha left home to become Sister Teresa in 1928, all surviving members of her immediate family had moved away, and she would not see her birthplace again for more than forty years.

Today Skopje, with a population of 400,000, is the third largest city in Yugoslavia and the capital of the Republic of Macedonia. Unvanquished by centuries of misfortunes, this proud city has known some considerable changes since that day in 1928 when the young Gonxha left it. The hands of the station clock, which remain frozen since 26 July 1963 at 5:17 a.m., attest to the most catastrophic of these changes: an earthquake which within five seconds killed 1,070 people and made another 140,000 homeless. Although the city had known many earthquakes throughout its history, this was by far the most devastating. It was enough to exorcise the town of all its furies, human and natural. One wonders if Mother Teresa recognized Skopje on her recent return to her native soil. Rebuilt by a Japanese architect, it is a new city today, with an enormous industrial complex, seven-story apartment blocks, and twenty skyscrapers with thirteen floors.

Nevertheless, the fifteenth-century cupolas of the Daut Pacha baths, which now house the Art Gallery, are still there. So too is the Church of the Holy Savior, with its magnificent wooden bell tower and courtyard outside, and inside a superb bishop's throne, pulpit, and iconostasis, on which are engraved marvelous icons inspired by the Old and New Tes-

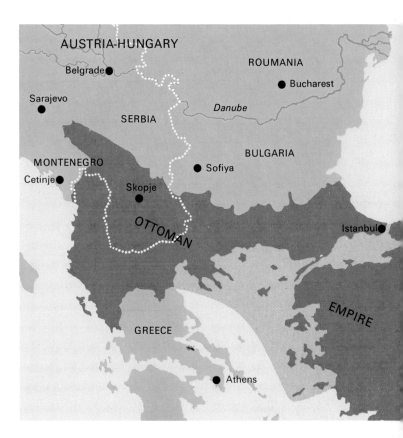

taments. Undoubtedly, Mother Teresa was aware that this church was dug into the ground because the Turks, who occupied the area for five centuries, did not want any place of worship other than a mosque to be visible to the naked eye. Undoubtedly also, the woman who would one day serve the poor of India admired the town's imperial gateway, where master woodcarvers engraved protraits of themselves seated at their workbenches.

MOSQUES AND CHURCHES IN TERESA'S HOMELAND

Also still standing in Skopje, although damaged in 1963, is the noble sixteenth-century fortress erected by the Byzantines, which dominates the city. From its lofty heights, one can see as far as the mountains, above the Vardar River, which 240 miles away empties itself in Greece—whose border is only 100 miles from Skopje—in the Gulf of Salonika. Opposite is the Mustafa Pacha Dzamija. Today this monument of fifteenth-century Ottoman art is a forum where craftsmen and merchants, Moslems, Albanians, and Gypsies sit in their stalls and shops, their darkened booths strangely surrounded by an even gloomier labyrinth of storefronts, all bearing the sign "Lawyer." On the left bank of the Vardar are other mosques, the most famous of which are Yahaja Pacha, Murat II, Aladza—names which must still reverberate in the memory of Mother Teresa like the words of a nursery rhyme. Did she ever travel the famous route of monasteries which leads from Skopje and forms a loop some 25 miles long? Since Mother Teresa has always been quite miserly in dispensing details of her childhood and adolescence, we will probably never know. At least we can speculate about whether she ever heard of Saint Nikita, with its stone-and-brick walls and its interior superbly decorated with frescoes depicting the Marriage at Canae and Christ chasing the moneylenders out of the temple. Or did she know the monasteries of the Virgin, the Annunciation, the Most Sanctified Elias—all with their painted façades—or Bogorodice, or the Archangel Gabriel? Perhaps she knew Nikole Sisuvski, accessible only to experienced climbers because of its situation next to the lake formed by the modern Matka dam and a verdant gorge.

Perhaps only asceticism would make it easy to detach oneself from these places, which must have made a permanent mark on Mother Teresa's childhood. Nor would it have been easy to escape the history of her country. Today this country is called Yugoslavia.

Contemporary Yugoslavia is such a cross-section of languages, ethnic groups, nationalities, and faiths that it is like a

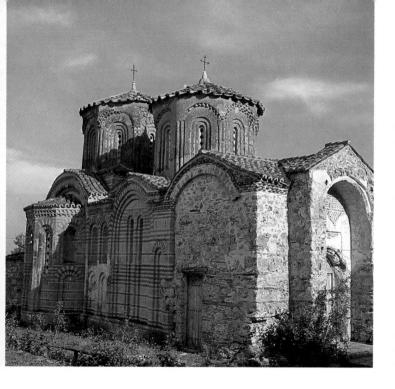

kaleidoscopic mosaic—if not a Tower of Babel. Agnes's family were Albanians, of which there remain no fewer than one million in Yugoslavia. Colonized by the Greeks, these people of mountaineer and peasant stock were in turn citizens of the Kingdoms of Epirus, Macedonia, and Bulgaria. In the eleventh century, Byzantium took control of Albania, causing many of its inhabitants to flee in the hope of avoiding the worst. Having found refuge in Macedonia, they found themselves exploited for many years by the same barbarian hordes they had sought to escape. They lived as a community alongside other communities—Turkish, Gypsy, Greek, Slav—in this area which was, under Tito, destined to become one of the six Republics composing Yugoslavia, and which was

traditionally a juncture of East and West, Cross and Crescent. From the earliest times countless tribes have coveted it. Illyrians, Greeks, Celts, Romans, Avars, Huns, and Hungarians fought over it, annexed it, colonized it, and rejected it throughout centuries of furious, incessant struggle. And finally they abandoned it to the wars which, naturally, left permanent scars.

Teresa also learned in her catechism about the two brothers, Cyril and Method, who coming to the region from Salonika in the ninth century, not only brought the first rudiments of the Christian faith but also translated the Bible into Slavonic. Five centuries of Turkish domination obviously left an imprint on the nation. From 1371, the Sublime Porte was mistress of Macedonia, and many times resisting forces tried to cast off the yoke of her oppression. On 3 August 1903—the feast day of St. Elie—seven years before Gonxha's birth, in Krusevo, a town not far from Skopje, the Revolutionary Interior Organization (VMRO) proclaimed a Republic. A Republic which was only to last 10 days. Immediately a terrifying and barbarous reign of repression was unleashed. Thus ended the attempt at an independent Macedonia.

The first Balkan War broke out between 1912 and 1913, when Agnes was three years old. Macedonia was taken from the Turks and divided up among the Greeks, Serbs, and Bulgarians. From 1920 to 1925, when Agnes was in the middle of adolescence, the Bulgarians stirred up trouble in the region and took advantage of their alliance with Germany to annex the country. This annexation lasted until the fall of the Nazis. If this area was a mosaic of race, it was also one of religion. As a souvenir of the long Turkish presence, Yugoslavia has 2,000 mosques; and Skopje alone, 365! In fact, we are not certain how many there are exactly, since no one has ever counted. Nor do we know how many Moslems there are. Possibly there are more than two million, but we have no recent statistics. At any rate, they are the third-ranking religious group, after eight million Orthodox and six million Catholics. It is significant that a secondary school expressly for the education of Islamic youth has recently opened in Skopje. At least this is a sign that, since Tito, Islam is considered a nationality. "The goal of this project," explained Henri Fesquet, "would be, on the one hand, to reduce the numbers of Croats (Catholics) and Serbs (Orthodox) as well as their excesses, and, on the other hand, to do credit to the religious sentiments of a part of the population; Islam being by far the most manageable of the three faiths." The Orthodox are quite well entrenched, especially in Serbia, as their two hundred monasteries attest.

The Catholics, who represent 37 percent of the population, are mostly concentrated in Slovenia and Croatia. They have closely adhered to an old-fashioned style, which is, by the way, the one in which Gonxha Bojaxhiu was brought up. In the seminaries, students are still not allowed to go out, and they live according to anti-Conciliar rites. It is a very traditional church; one that runs no risk of begetting one of those neo-theologians who make Rome tremble. That Mother Teresa has remained attached to this tradition is shown by her way of life, of prayer, and of judging changing customs.

One wonders whether she felt out of her element when she arrived in India—this immense country, so rich in contrasts, gigantic in every way, a veritable complex of populations, languages, and religions. Her childhood had prepared her for it. Indeed, so had the history of her country taught her to fight, just as the revolutionaries of her native Macedonia had fought in all the dark years of their occupation.

TWO SISTERS

How different from her present life—her daily work in Calcutta among the poor and sick and dying—is this view of Gonxha Bojaxhiu and her sister Aga in their young womanhood in Yugoslavia so long ago.

But if the picture has survived, like some archaeological artifact from a civilization long disappeared, it is difficult today to find anyone who can identify all the figures it shows. We know only that Gonxha (Teresa) is the young woman seated in the second row and that her sister Aga, five years older, is standing, with the parasol, beside her.

The two sisters were, from all accounts, very close. Despite their age difference they had a great deal in common, particularly their love of music. The two girls were pillars of their church choir and of the Skopje Albanian youth choir. Lorenz Antoni, a successful composer of Albanian extraction living in Yugoslavia today, recalls the regular concerts given by this group between 1926 and 1928 when he was still, like Gonxha, a high school student. She was a regular soloist.

Aga, the eldest child, was the most serious. Extremely intelligent, more bookish than Gonxha, she was also more successful in her studies. She completed the Skopje high school with a specialization in economics and went on, when Gonxha became a nun, to work as a milliner in Albania, where she went to live with her widowed mother in 1928.

Thenceforth Aga spent the next forty years in complete devotion to her mother. The two women remained in Albania until their death, cut off by an isolated, xenophobic government from all contact with the world beyond their narrow borders. Teresa could occasionally exchange a letter by relay through Italy, but not at all on a regular basis.

How could Aga and her mother, with their strict and devout Catholicism, fare in this rigorous, rigid orthodox Marxist society that accused the Soviet Union and even China of bourgeois revisionism? Whatever the nature of their accommodation to this society, they seem to have managed to survive, and even to prosper. Aga's native gifts and her sound early education brought her a good position in postwar Albania as a journalist and a broadcaster on Radio Tirana. The mother lived to the age of eighty-three, and died in Tirana in 1968. Aga survived her mother by only three years.

HER BROTHER REMEMBERS...

Mother Teresa's only surviving relative, her brother Lazar Bojaxhiu, has been largely neglected by authors and journalists writing about Teresa. His appearance by her side at Oslo in December 1979 came therefore as something of a surprise. Mr. Bojaxhiu, now seventy-two, an Italian resident since World War II, maintains close ties with Teresa and meets her whenever possible. In an exclusive interview, he shared with us his memories of their childhood and family life in Skopje, and discussed his feelings about his world-famous sister.

*   *   *

In 1928, Lieutenant Lazar Bojaxhiu learned to his dismay that his younger sister Gonxha had decided to become a nun. "Shocked, I wrote her a letter. I had been away from home

and had scarcely seen the family in six years. This news was completely unexpected. My sister had always been so lively, so healthy, a pretty child, mischievous and hearty. 'How could *you*,' I wrote to her, 'a girl like *you*, become a nun? Do you realize that you are burying yourself?'

"I will never forget her answer. We had not exchanged letters

before. I had just been promoted to lieutenant, on completing military academy in Albania, and was very full of myself. Gonxha wrote me, 'You think you are so important, as an official serving the king of two million subjects. Well, I am an official too, serving the King of the whole world. Which one of us is right?'

"But as time went by, and I thought more about her decision, her vocation, I wasn't really surprised after all. To understand this, you have know something about our family background, our life in Skopje under very special circumstances, and the role that the Church had always played in Albanians' lives.

"When my parents married, around 1900 in the city of Prizren, Albania as a country did not even exist. But an independence movement *did* exist, very much so. And my father was a patriot, very active in the movement both in Prizren and later, when he married and moved to Skopje in Yugoslavia. Albanians had always known foreign occupation and exile. But we held together, kept our language and our traditions alive. Some Albanians were Moslems, some Orthodox, but my family, for generations and generations, had been Catholic. And it was the Catholic Church that kept us going, kept us together.

"My father was political, my mother more religious. And

Lazar Bojaxhiu, two years older than Teresa, is often seen with his famous sister during her visits to Europe. He and his daughter were at Teresa's side in Oslo for the Nobel ceremony, and the pictures at left show the brother and sister in Rome when the Missionaries of Charity were received by Pope Paul VI. Has Teresa changed since those long-ago childhood days? "Very little," says her brother.

As a child, according to her brother, Teresa was plump, mischievous, fun-loving, and a real tomboy.

The snapshot below shows the more serious adolescent she was to become, after the sudden death of her father (when she was not yet ten) brought harder times for the whole family. Seen here in black, Gonxha was a studious, hard-working girl who coached her classmates after school and spent every available hour at church. She showed an early enthusiasm for foreign missions—her priest spoke often of the Loreto Order and its work in India. She loved music, had a fine voice, and excelled in performances of the local choir.

while I followed in my father's footsteps, my sister Aga [born in 1905] and Gonxha [Teresa, born 1912] took after my mother. But I am getting ahead of my story. First I have to correct some of the misinformation that has been printed about Mother Teresa and her family in recent years.

"Some books and magazines call Mother Teresa a 'peasant.' Completely false. I read that my father was a grocer, a druggist. False again. Some reports even claim that Mother Teresa never had a brother!

"My father was co-owner, with an Italian friend, of a construction firm in Skopje, and quite successful. Until his death, in terrible circumstances, we were well off and lacked for nothing. He owned two houses with gardens, and we lived in one of them. I was the middle child, two years older than Gonxha. There were other girls in the family, but they both died very young.

"The house was always full of visitors as long as my father lived. Albanian nationalists, political allies. There was constant talk of our country and its independence from foreign domination.

"One night my father came home from a political meeting complaining that he felt ill. He collapsed and began to hemorrhage. He was rushed to the hospital and died in surgery. It was all over in a matter of hours. I am convinced that he was poisoned, for political reasons.

"Thus—he died in 1919—changed everything, overnight. What would have become of us without my mother, I don't know. I feel that we owe her everything. I would like to erect a great monument to this woman. She had been used to a comfortable life, and now suddenly she had nothing. She worked wonders. To support us, she organized an embroidery handcraft business. She saw that we kept our home, stayed together, and went to school. She was a marvelous woman, and probably even outshone my father. She was less garrulous and outgoing, less involved in causes, but just as effective as he.

"One cause was important to her, of course: the Church. I remember how serious we were about our Catholicism, how strict and active we were. Organizing prayer groups, special observances, May Day ceremonies. We lived near the church

The transformation of this warm and affectionate young woman into a nun was at first difficult for her brother to believe or accept. For more than thirty years they did not meet, and the portrait at right stayed with him as a reminder of a Gonxha who had ceased to exist. Their reunion in Rome in 1952 was a chance to get acquainted all over again, and today the brother and sister are closer than ever. She writes regularly to Lazar in their native Albanian language, but the signature is now "M. Teresa": her new identity is complete. And significantly Lazar, like everyone else, calls her "Mother."

—the Albanians' Catholic church of Skopje, which had an Albanian priest when we were children. Sometimes my mother and sisters seemed to live *at* church. The choir, the services, and later all the talk about missions....

"One incident I have never forgotten. In those days, before taking Holy Communion you had to fast from midnight on —you weren't allowed to eat or drink anything. And one Saturday night, as a small boy, I woke up in the night, or early morning, and took a drink of water. Then I remembered! I ended up going to my mother in tears to confess what I had done. She took it very seriously and said we would have to go to the priest that morning before Mass and explain that I could not receive Communion that day. I still remember the—the holy terror I felt on realizing what I had done. Just compare this with the way Catholics go to Communion today.

"Where our house had been a hotbed of political discussions while my father lived, after his death it was more of a religious center. And this shows you how Teresa became Teresa: why she became a nun in the first place. Our mother was unusually religious, the girls were always organizing church activities and choir singing, and we constantly tried to help people. My mother was interested in missions, and she would take in local people too and feed and help them.

"I remember when my mother found out about a poor woman in Skopje who had a tumor and had no one to care for her. Her family refused to help or even to give her shelter. My mother brought this woman to live in our house. With all her other responsibilities, my mother housed and fed the woman and cared for her until she got well. So you see, 'Teresa' did not just spring out of the blue.

"Gonxha [Teresa], by age thirteen, when I left home, was already fascinated by mission work. She loved to meet returning missionaries and hear their accounts of work in the field. She seemed to remember every detail. Once, at a church meeting when Gonxha was twelve or thirteen, our new parish priest, a Jesuit, showed a map of the world with missions indicated on it. Gonxha amazed everyone by going up to the map and explaining the activities and exact location of every one of the missions. The priest was very impressed, and of course he continued to encourage her interest during the next several years. His order was related to the Loreto Sisters, which Gonxha eventually joined.

"So it was really not so hard, after all, to understand Gonxha's wanting to become a nun. All I have to do, really, is think of my mother and her complete devotion to the Church. And, you know, we were very disciplined Catholics in our house, as I told you. That same discipline is the backbone of Mother Teresa's order, the Missionaries of Charity, today. It is a very strict order, you know, carefully organized, with a real hierarchy. I told her, 'You are something of an army officer yourself, just like me. You must have done military training! Your are like the commander of a military base or a fleet.'

"There is a fantastic strength in her, just like my mother and sister. A force of character.

"It must have cost our mother a lot to let Gonxha go so far away to join the Loreto Sisters. And never to see her again. But there was no going back. They both knew the decision had been the right one."

HER JOURNEY TO THE POOREST OF ALL

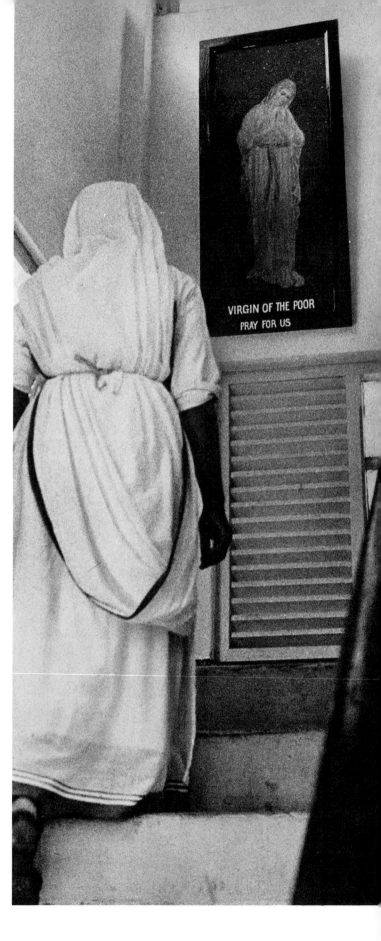

VIRGIN OF THE POOR
PRAY FOR US

On 29 November 1928 young Gonxha arrived in Dublin. She had come, on her way to India, to learn English at the principal convent of Loreto, the congregation she had decided to join. This institute was founded in the seventeenth century by Mary Ward with the aim of educating young girls. Its rules were based on those of the Society of Jesus, and its spirituality entirely on the famous *Spiritual Exercises,* which Ignatius of Loyola, the founder of the Jesuits, had made the cornerstone of his Order.

Being a soldier, Ignatius of Loyola did not mince words. His *Exercises,* a tidy little hundred-page book, is divided into four parts, the last constituting a series of rules on intellectual perception, the distribution of alms, and on scruples. In twenty

Jesus said, "I am hungry, I am naked, I am homeless."
By serving the poor, I am serving Him.... Actually we are
touching Christ's body in the poor. In the poor it is
the hungry Christ that we are feeding, it is the naked
Christ that we are clothing, it is the homeless Christ that
we are giving shelter.... When I wash that leper's wounds,
I feel I am nursing the Lord himself.

lines he summed up the meaning of life and the Christian experience, before beginning on the exercises which are intended to last for four weeks.

The first week is devoted to final ends, to sin, and to Hell; the second, to the "choice" that everyone must make for a total fidelity to the life of Christ. The last two aim at confirming men in their commitment to their chosen way of life, by first meditating on the Passion of Jesus and then on the Resurrection. The third part of the book, called "Meditations," is a sequence of dry formulas, a thorough treaty on spirituality. These exercises appeal to the intelligence; there is an absence of all sensibility. Austerity and abstraction are the basis of this moral treatise. It is expressed in terms of a combat, and it is in this quasi-military sense that we must understand the term "Exercise."

The culmination of these four weeks of retreat is found on the fourth day of the second week, in the famous meditation on the "two banners," in which St. Ignatius shows two enemy armies confronting each other: that of Christ "in the Kingdom of Jerusalem," with all his followers: and, in the Kingdom of Babylon, that commanded by Satan, who is "seated on a kind of throne of fire and smoke." The true Christian is someone who has made Christ a gift of his faith and who fights for him. His offensive weapon is the examination of the conscience, twice a day, which overcomes all vices.

It is, then, a strict, rigorous discipline, and no lapses are tolerated. This notion of a combat is the key to Ignatius' spirituality. And the combat has but one goal: the glory of God, "Ad majoram Dei gloriam." This famous phrase recurs constantly in the writings of Ignatius, some thousand times in his correspondence and his works, 104 times in the Constitutions of his Order. Nothing else really mattered to him. No wonder then that as an introduction to his book of *Exercises*, he inscribed these words: "Man is created to praise, venerate, and serve Our Lord and by this means to save his soul." Such prodding cannot fail to lead adepts to the highest summits of mystical experience by way of prayer and contemplation. It is understandable that these exercises inspired so many saints and founders of religious orders, including Mary Ward and Teresa of Calcutta herself.

It was a long journey from Skopje to Calcutta, with various stops along the way. But it was not yet over when she arrived in Calcutta: she had not yet reached the poorest of the poor. "Virgin of the Poor, pray for us" reads the wall poster (left) which Teresa passed every day in the convent of the Sisters of Loreto; a poster that must have influenced the young nun. Today, another poster hangs in the Home for the Dying Destitute which Teresa founded. Its motto motivates her and her missionaries in their ongoing journey.

In the beginning, the congregation of Loreto went through every imaginable difficulty, just like the Society of Jesus, and it was suppressed by Pope Urban VIII in 1631, though he reinstated the Order a few years later. But it was not until 1703 that the Sisters of Loreto received the approval of Pope Clement XI. By that time the Order had opened houses in Germany and Austria. Somewhat later (in 1821) the house in Dublin was founded. And this Irish chapter, situated at Rathfarnham, Dublin, where Teresa arrived in 1928, had established congregations in Australia, Canada (28 houses), and the United States (12 houses).

Today the congregation has ten thousand members and houses on five continents. The sisters, called variously "Ladies of Loreto," "Le Dame Inglesi," "Die englischen Fräulein," or the "Loreto Nuns," teach classes ranging from first grade to university and, above all, prepare girls for their future role as lay apostles in the world.

The congregation was born in the seventeenth century—which the French historian Daniel-Rops has named "the great century of souls"—when Saint Francis of Sales was diffusing the teachings of the Abbé Brémond under the title of "devout humanism." St. Francis, apostle of gentleness, died six years before Mary Ward even conceived of founding her Order, having spread the idea that humility is a virtue because it is consecrated by God. Man, he claimed, is attracted to light. He has no choice but a life of devotion. *Devoted, devout, devotion*—these words had greater meaning in those days. This was also the age of the French school of spirituality: Cardinal Bérulle, with the aid of Madame Acarie, established the Carmelites, reformed by Teresa of Avila in France.

First stop for the eighteen-year-old Albanian postulant: Rathfarnham, Dublin, home of the Sisters of Loreto, where she arrived for a two-month stay on 29 November 1928. Mother Francis Xavier (left), who was also a young nun at the time, recalls Teresa as a shy, solitary person struggling to learn English.

He was to have a profound influence on St. Vincent de Paul, a precursor of Teresa of Calcutta. This was the age of St. Jean-Eudes, founder of the Bon Pasteur Order devoted to the rehabilitation of prostitutes; of Monsieur Olier, the priest of St. Sulpice and founder of the Society of the same name, who trained teachers for seminaries. It was also the age of the flourishing of religious Orders. The era of Bernini and the Colonnade of St. Peter was soon to arrive. In England the Stuarts reigned and Anglicans were pitted against Catholics.

And so Teresa arrived in Ireland, a country that Bernard Shaw described as primarily a climate. It is a cool and damp climate, the first European point exposed to the western winds, a place with shifting and capricious skies. In this country it is possible to have the four seasons in one day, a "tear and a smile" in succession. Dublin, resplendent with superb parks, is profoundly affected by the memory of the Celts and the Norman Conquerors, not to mention Cromwell and the Georgian era, which left pompous monuments

This chapter of the "Ladies of Loreto" order, founded in 1821, has divisions in Spain, Australia, and other countries including India. In the photograph at left, we see the main gate leading to the three-story Georgian convent building. Below right: The refectory and dormitory of the school that is operated at Rathfarnham.

herself understood in this country where she felt a bit like an exile. Some of the nuns such as Mother Victorine, who was a novice with her, or Mother Francis Xavier, remember her as a young postulant "very small, quiet, and shy." Her only friend was a postulant who was a compatriot of hers. Another nun recalls that she would answer anyone who found her devotion remarkable, "I could never face God if I didn't do this work." Surprisingly there are no anecdotes. "What is remarkable," says one of her former comrades, "is that she was ordinary."

Teresa has not forgotten Rathfarnham. On several occasions

and austere dwellings. Jonathan Swift and Oscar Wilde were born there and so were Nobel Prize laureates such as George Bernard Shaw, Samuel Becket, and James Joyce. Twelve years before Teresa's arrival, Irish nationalists, in 1916, taking advantage of the difficulties the English were having in a war on the continent, led a rebellion which was crushed severely.

In this land of contrasts, a change from her native Yugoslavia, Teresa hardly spent two months. She has not left many traces. She did not speak English, and thus she had trouble making

she has returned there as if on a pilgrimage. She even sent her Missionaries to Belfast in the Ballymurphy district in the spirit of ecumenism—albeit without lasting success. Today she maintains such close ties with Loreto that she uses the same congregation of her own novitiate to train the novices of the Missionaries of Charity. It suffices to say that she has never repudiated her first years of training as a young nun. She seems to feel she owes everything to Loreto.

DARJEELING

It was in the "city of lightning," with its population of 40,000, perched at an altitude of 7,000 feet, that this young postulant arrived one day in 1929. There she found the novitiate of the Sisters of Loreto, at the foot of the Kanchenjunga, a giant of the Himalayas whose highest point capped in eternal snow is less than 60 miles away as the crow flies. On the other side lies Tibet. Founded by the English as a summer capital in 1816, Darjeeling was the site of a privileged summer residence for the governor of Bengal and his staff, as well as for well-off families fleeing the humid heat of Calcutta 300 miles away. Theirs was a fairytale existence: excursions on horseback, dinners at the Gymkhana club, *thés dansants* on the lawn of Government House.

The city is in tiers ranging in altitude from 7,002 to 7,139 feet. At the lowest part is found the bazaar, a meeting point of all the races. The higher part overlooks the jungle, where tigers, deer, and elephants roam wild. Six miles away is Tiger Hill (7,500 feet) from which Teresa might once have seen the sun rise over one of the highest summits of the world.

It was here, on 24 May 1931, after two years as a novice, that Gonxha took her first vows and chose the name Teresa in memory of Theresa of Avila and, even more, little Teresa of Lisieux. Then she was sent to St. Mary's School for Girls run by the Loreto sisters in Entally, a district of Calcutta. While teaching history and geography there, she discovered Calcutta, long known as the cesspool of the world. And there, one day in 1946, her real vocation was revealed to her. This was the date she was to name her "day of decision," her "second vocation."

Early in 1929, direct from Ireland, Teresa reached the Loreto convent in Darjeeling, a mountain resort town in north India that was popular with the British colonialists. The Loreto sisters did not come in contact with the poorer elements seen in the bottom of the picture at right, but taught the daughters of the rich. Teresa took her first vows in Darjeeling on 24 May 1931, but was already assigned to a teaching post in Calcutta. The sisters in Calcutta lived in the fine building shown on the opposite page.

CALCUTTA

Calcutta participates in the realest sense in Christ's passion. It is sad to see so much misery in our beloved Calcutta. But Calcutta will rise again to become the Mother of the Poor.

"Calcutta is like an obscene and surrealistic photo-montage, juxtaposing poverty and opulence, different races and castes, and to cite two extreme examples, Victorian palaces and reed huts of 'bastis'—the local name for shantytowns." Thus a tourist guidebook describes this man-eating city, which seems about to burst at its seams. It is the capital of Western Bengal and the intellectual capital of all India. This city of eight million is a veritable phenomenon where wealth and poverty meet; where the two goddesses Kali, divinity of destruction and death, and Sarasvati, protector of Arts and Letters, vie for the devotion of pious souls; and where one of the greatest poets of modern times, Rabindranath Tagore—not to mention Ramakrishna—made his home. Created out of the junction of three villages, it was made a colony by the English in the eighteenth century. Its colonial past is still evident in the Victorian buildings that surround Dalhousie Square in the

33

neighborhood of Alipore, where the wealthiest families live today. Not far from here is Teresa's Home for the Dying. Walking down these streets, you would imagine that this is a holy place of pilgrimage, so numerous are the merchants of religious articles. Their stalls are filled with the colored statuettes that the pilgrims decorate with garlands of flowers before throwing them into the Hooghly, the river flowing through the city. From June to October, the monsoon, however much it has been hoped for, transforms the slums into a veritable quagmire. As is well known, when the British withdrew from the subcontinent, three nations were formed: India, Pakistan, and Ceylon. This partition, which took place in 1947, drove thousands of refugees into the city. And what is more, every year peasants from the west also arrive in droves only to aggravate an already endemic ill: unemployment.

In this country one has the impression of being permanently in the presence of a divine spirit, so closely are daily lives here entwined with the various indigenous religions. Divinities abound. There are all kinds in all places. The most famous are Brahma, Vishnu, and Shiva. Their Bible, the Ramayana, whose 24,000 verses go back to the third or fourth century

before Christ, was according to legend written by the prophet Vahmiki at the bidding of the god Brahma. There are also 17 million Christians, most of whom live in the south and are descended from "untouchables" whom missionaries converted, entire villages at a time, in the thirteenth and fourteenth centuries.

Teresa got to know the language, along with the place, discovering these miserable bands of beggars and lepers sleeping right out on the sidewalks—a spectacle which is at once fascinating and repugnant—in the middle of burlap factories, cotton manufacturers, metallurgy, chemical and pharmaceutical works, and other mills.

charmers attract passersby along the Jawaharlal Nehru Road, aswarm with movie theaters and their gaudy marquees. In front of boutiques and shops beggars lie prostrate.

At the gate of the Marble Palace there are again beggars plying their trade. Inside stands the palace, constructed in 1835 in the heart of a poverty-stricken area. Teresa and her sisters have settled here not far from the zoo and the national library, which is the former residence of the Indian viceroys, surrounded by sumptuous gardens. For twenty years Teresa ran all over Calcutta. She rubbed shoulders with the poorest of the city, all the time performing perfectly her obligatory service: teaching the wealthy students of St. Mary's.

A rare photograph of Teresa in the happy life she gave up at St. Mary's High School. She loved teaching, loved her students, but could not close her eyes forever to the suffering that began just outside her window. Indeed, the slums of Moti Jheel (right), directly beside St. Mary's, were visible from the school, a constant reminder that she was surrounded by neighbors less fortunate than herself and her young students.

It is perhaps because Calcutta has one of the highest average per capita incomes in the country, after Delhi and Bombay, that the peasants, driven from their land by insufficient rainfall or from borrowing at usurious rates (the interest rate is not regulated), flee en mass to this city with its stifling, humid climate. Here fakirs, monkey trainers, and snake

St. Mary's, with its huge protective wall, is an opulent no man's land situated at the gates of suffering and squalor. From her room, Teresa looked straight down into the slums of Moti Jheel, where whole families were heaped together. The contrast was a dramatic revelation to her: her life was never to be the same again.

THE VOCATION

On 10 September 1946, Teresa reached a crossroads in her life. On the train which was taking her to Darjeeling, she heard a call from God: "a second calling," she named it later, "a call within my Vocation." The message, she later explained, was clear: "to give up even Loreto where I was very happy and to go out in the streets. I heard the call to give up all and follow Christ into the slums to serve him among the poorest of the poor. I had first to apply to the Archbishop of Calcutta." A nun must in fact obtain permission to live outside of the convent even though she remains bound by the perpetual vows she has taken. This was the case with Teresa. It is no simple formality to create an Order. Rome is always hesitant to authorize a new Foundation. Indeed there are innumerable feminine institutions which—and this is truer today than formerly—having had a very strong recruitment, end up by fading out for lack of vocations. Edward Le Joly, who was for twenty years the spiritual adviser to the Missionaries of Charity, has filled in the rest of the story.

The archbishop of Calcutta had asked Teresa if she had the physical and spiritual capability to carry out her proposed vocation: did she really know what she was asking of herself? There were some doubts, too, about how she would be accepted by the people. This was 1946, the eve of Indian independence. A European woman, dressed like an Indian, working in the slums at the head of a group of Bengali girls, might expect to meet considerable opposition. The archbishop decided to take a chance and let her try.

And so on 16 August 1948 she left Loreto and began her work. It was work which from the very beginning, represented a major challenge. Asked if she has ever had any doubts about her vocation, Mother Teresa invariably answers, "No, I have never doubted. I am at God's disposal. Without him I can do nothing."

Suddenly, in 1946, while on a train journey, Teresa felt in the clearest terms the call to leave her school and devote herself to the poor and suffering. But was it really like a bolt from the blue? She had always been aware of struggles going on out on the streets, of which this photograph offers one painful example.

Our Lord wants me to be a free nun, covered with the poverty of the Cross. But today I learned a great lesson. The poverty of the poor must be so hard for them. When looking for a center, I walked and walked until my legs and arms ached. I thought how much they must ache in soul and body looking for a home, food, and health. Then the comfort of Loreto came to tempt me, but of my own free choice, my God, and out of love for you, I desire to remain and do whatever be your holy will in my regard. Give me courage now, this moment.

THE HAND OF MOTHER TERESA

It is not enough for us to say: I love God, but I do not love my neighbor. St. John says you are a liar if you say you love God and you don't love your neighbor. How can you love God whom you do not see, if you do not love your neighbor whom you see, whom you touch, with whom you live. And so this is very important for us to realize that love, to be true, has to hurt. It hurt Jesus to love us, it hurt him.

This child supported by Mother Teresa's firm but gentle hand captures far better than words the tenderness of a woman whose ministry, and whose whole life, is an abiding gift of herself. And what inestimable comfort this hand has provided, and still provides. A hand that strokes a child's forehead or that of a dying person, offers food to the destitute, relieves suffering as well as solitude. It is a hand extended for the love of others, generous, fruitful, powerful, strong, sublime. In the child's face we read infinite gratitude, the light of grace, ecstactic joy. Other hands are useless, if not harmful, but Teresa's bless, pacify, and protect. They are a refuge, like the hands of God. Péguy was right when he said: "The spiritual is itself carnal." Indeed Teresa's prayers spring from a most womanly heart, and miracles from her hands.

Miraculous is the word that best describes this great woman of the poor, who had once been so tranquil within her convent and whose life was so perfectly routinized, smooth-running, secure, and peaceful.

But now Sister Teresa was launched on an adventure, leaving her sisters as though she were leaving her home and family. Here she was all of a sudden, left to her own devices, to a kind of solitude, deprived of the support of her circle of loved ones. "Leaving Loreto was for me the greatest sacrifice, the most difficult thing I have ever done. It was a lot more difficult than leaving my family and country to become a nun. Loreto was everything to me." This is an astonishing confession, for she is so entirely devoted to God that one might almost believe her to be detached from everything earthly. Yet it was far from easy for her to tear herself away from those who loved her. However, having taken the plunge, she never looked back, but forged bravely ahead.

If not for her steadfast faith and her almost innate trust in God, she might have renounced her undertaking.

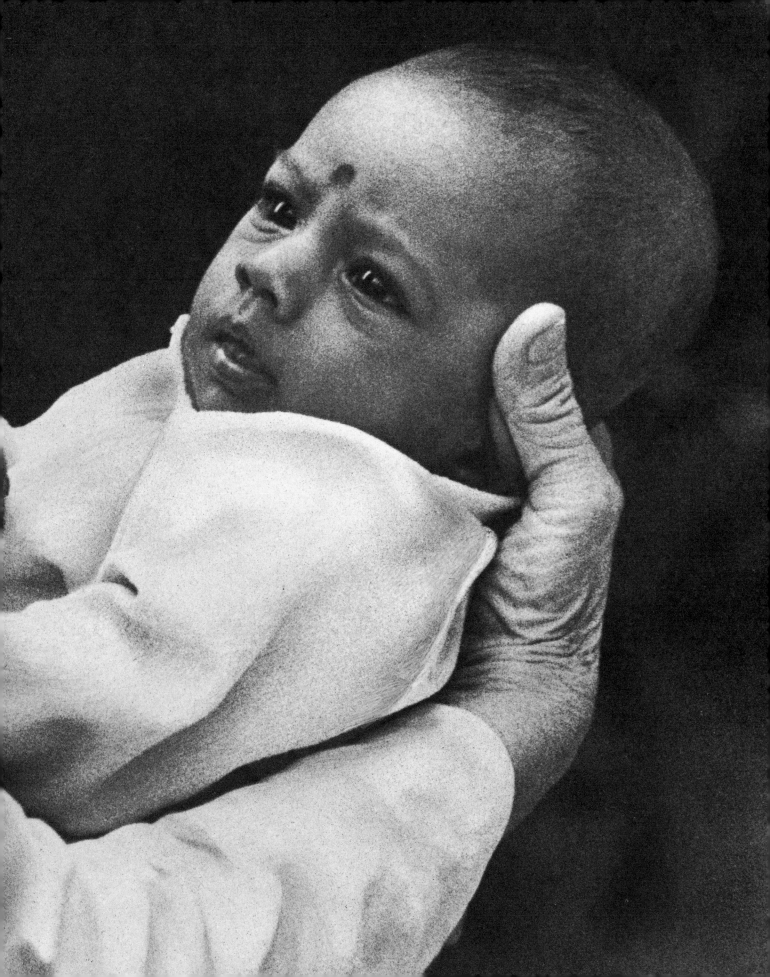

STARTING FROM NOTHING

She left Calcutta to spend some time in Patna, a city four hundred miles away situated on the right bank of the Ganges. Patna, founded in the sixth century B.C., was the seat of the famous king Asoka, unifier of India. For three months, Mother Teresa lived in this university town of a half-million inhabitants, where she took a nursing course with the American medical missionary sisters. This is an indispensable education for someone wanting to devote herself to the care of the poor, to attend to their basic health needs.

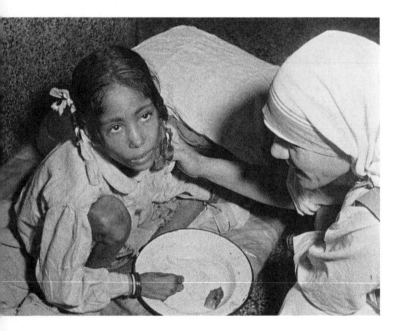

Church at that time revolutionary. What then, we may ask, was so surprising about Teresa's proposal? For one thing, she demanded of those who would join her that they live strictly and adhere to a more than spartan existence. We need only cite one example: her insistence on a bare regimen of rice and vegetables. (She was eventually persuaded to give it up.)

In the year 1948, when Teresa was thirty-eight years old, Pius XII responded favorably to her request to leave the Congregation of Loreto to live as an independent nun. It was then that she wore her new habit for the first time: a white sari with a blue border. She returned to Calcutta, and began her great undertaking. Here in the slums of Matizhil, among hovels in the corner of a private garden, was the haven that she rented for five rupees a month.

She won her first campaign by doing what she knew best, teaching. But this time her students were not rich young girls

One day she announced to the missionary nuns directing the school her plan to change her life in order to be reunited with the poor, to identify herself with them almost physically. But to do it she would need to create a congregation entirely devoted to this apostolate. Her proposal astonished, even disturbed, the nuns. All except one: the superior of the school, Mother Dengel. She had herself once taken a big risk with some of her own innovations. She had asked for and obtained permission from the Holy See to open a surgical and gynecological service in her convent, a request which was for the

Teresa's first efforts were devoted to children (opposite page), whom she sought to feed, clothe, heal, and educate in her impromptu roving clinic-classrooms. If her beginning was difficult and lonely, Teresa was soon getting help. One form of assistance came in the form of housing put at her disposal by generous individuals and church officials. It was not long before she was organizing her many activities under one roof. The house seen at left, at 14 Creek Lane, became the dwelling place of Teresa's Missionaries of Charity in 1949.

Other help was also forthcoming in the form of volunteer helpers, young women eager to follow Teresa's example in devoting their lives to serving the poor. These women, many of them former students of Teresa, would eventually form the nucleus of her order the Missionaries of Charity, with congregations throughout India and the world. The Missionaries wear, like Teresa, the white sari with blue stripe (below) and lead an ascetic life, although she sees that they take adequate food and rest to survive their rigorous work day.

as at Loreto, but about thirty children whom, despite great odds, she strove to make literate. Her "school," for want of a better word, had no tables, no seats, and no blackboard. Not finding any other place on which to trace the daily lessons, Teresa knelt down on the bare earth, flattened out a patch of ground with her hand, and started writing with a stick. She took advantage of this system to teach the children such elementary hygiene as how to wash with a bar of soap. And for them a bar of soap is a royal luxury, something most of them had never seen. As soon as she finished the day's lessons, she would rush out to other squalid slums to visit sick people and to inquire after the needs of families.

For all that, she never neglected her duties as a nun. It was among the Little Sisters of the Poor that Teresa sought refuge to say her prayers. This congregation, founded by the Frenchwoman Jeanne Jugan, had the vocation of begging for the subsistence of two hundred old and indigent people who were quartered in their convent. With them Teresa felt at home: these Little Sisters of the Poor are in fact members of the same spiritual clan.

CHILDREN FROM OUT OF THE DUSTBIN

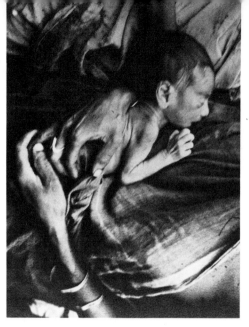

Sometimes we get three or more babies a day. Always one for sure. More than half the number die because they are premature. I think some mothers have taken drugs to get rid of the children which harm them: they are drugged and need a great deal of care. Still they struggle to live and some are able to survive. If they do, it is a miracle. Some weigh less than two pounds, they are unable to suck and must be fed through the nose or by injection until they are strong enough to suck.

Sister Agnes

The poor, the sick, the outcast are found at every stage of life, from the aged to the newest newborn infant.

Every morning a nun makes the rounds of the hospitals and rubbish heaps of Calcutta, rarely returning from this sinister excursion without a baby in her arms. The galloping population of India is an acute and insoluble problem even though the birthrate has been diminishing continually for sixty years (51.3 percent in 1911, 35.6 percent in 1974), and the mortality rate has declined even more (47.2 percent in 1911, 15.2 percent 1974). Some people have trouble accepting Teresa's savage hostility to abortion, and she responds: "God gives what is needed. He gives to the flowers, to the birds, and little children are his life. There are never enough of them. God made the world sufficiently rich to feed and clothe all human beings."

Even if one does not agree with her, who can fail to respect such an evangelical confidence? If most of these newborn babies gathered in by Mother Teresa only live a few hours, she takes charge of the rest, seeing to their upbringing either in her own schools or by finding them adoptive parents almost anywhere in the world.

Shishu Bhavan, a plain two-storied building in Calcutta, its

Countless infants left to die in clinics, on the street, and in garbage bins have survived thanks to the Missionaries of Charity. The children gathered in at the Missionaries' hospital Shishu Bhivan in Calcutta are seen at feeding time (opposite page) and resting on the floor (below). Those that survive will be placed in adoptive homes or kept in some of the Missionaries' eighty-seven orphanages in India.

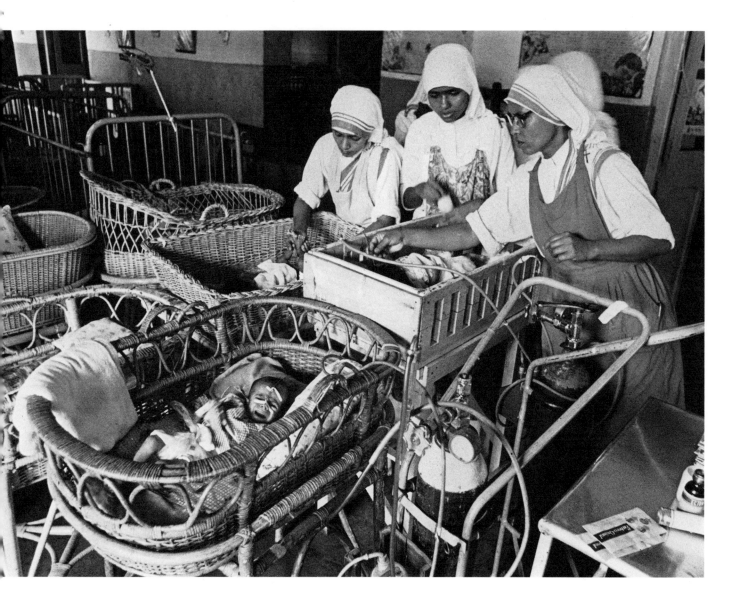

rough, unpainted outer walls covered with graffiti and a large cross, houses the home for children and several of the Missionaries' other diverse activities—soup kitchen, administrative office, clinic, dispensary, even a shelter for those young women who will bear the unwanted children of tomorrow— the homeless unwed mothers-to-be whom Teresa's people have taken in.

A visitor to the center will see people of all ages coming to be fed, and children everywhere. Inside Shishu Bhavan, his attention is likely to be drawn first and foremost to the tiny premature infants, almost unbelievably small, lying two or three to a bed, connected to various life support systems. Occasionally their plight is driven home to people living thousands of miles away. An Englishman in Surrey once described to us a meeting he attended of the Co-Workers of

Mother Teresa, where someone in the audience asked if he could contribute some baby clothing for the infants of Shishu Bhavan. "Yes," he was told. "You could knit or crochet some things—but remember, if you make hats for the babies, they should be the size of a tennis ball."

Heads the size of a tennis ball . . . It is scarcely surprising that so many of these premature infants seen in the center on a given day will have disappeared the next.

The survivors can often be placed in adoptive homes in the West, or even in India.

But there are more children being cared for than one sees in Shishu Bhavan. "We sponsor children. Say, a widow has five or six children; we sponsor one or two—the bright ones—so at least they will be able to help the family when they grow up. We see them through school," says Sister Agnes.

"A DISGRACE THAT PEOPLE ARE DYING IN THE STREETS"

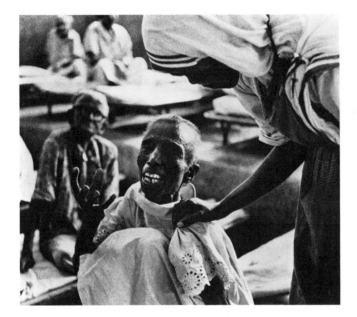

The year 1952 marked the opening of the first Home for the Dying. Every morning in Calcutta the dead bodies are carried out and the dying are collected. A persistent legend has it that it was after finding a woman in the street half eaten by rats and ants that the idea came to Teresa to found a home for those who are about to die. No one knew where to put this woman, and Teresa is said to have taken her to the City Hall in order to force the authorities to give her a place to gather in this human refuse. And then came the miracle—a miracle that was suddenly to make her famous.

In the picture above, a nun attends to a patient in the Nirmal Hriday Home for Dying Destitutes, Calcutta, founded by Teresa in 1952.
Right: *More recently the Missionaries of Charity opened another hospital for the dying in Calcutta when the industrial firm ICI gave them a large building and grounds. Here mentally ill patients are also housed (they are seen during mealtime in this picture), and a workshop has been installed. The place has been christened Prem Dam ("Gift of Love").*

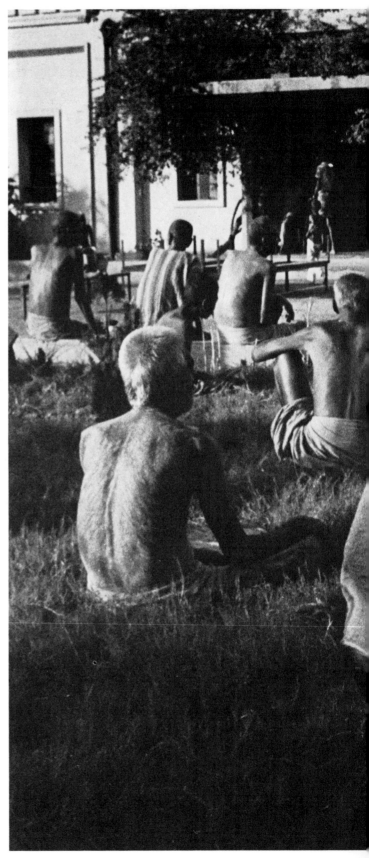

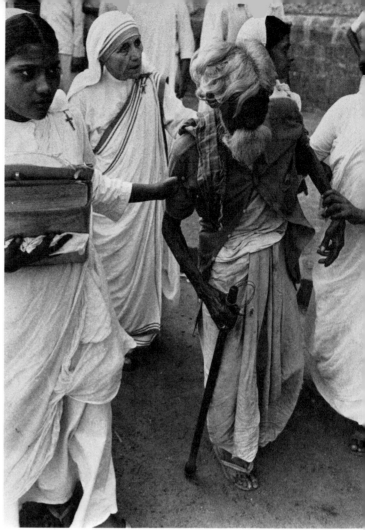

One of the public health officials brought her to the Temple of Kali, which was reconstructed in 1809 and lies along the Kalighar—a dried-up branch of the Hooghly River. Here she was shown the "darmashalah," where formerly the faithful would rest after doing their devotions to Kali. This Hindu goddess of death and destruction is especially venerated in Bengal and bloody sacrifices used to be offered in her honor. Now the "darmashalah" was abandoned and empty. Twenty-four hours later, Teresa, accompanied by her young recruits, occupied the place with their sick patients. They were greeted by the petrified and anxious stare of monks who were visibly less than happy at the arrival of these strange squatters. Nonetheless one of them took up her defense. "For thirty years I have been serving the Goddess Kali in the Temple," he said. "Today I see before me the 'Goddess-Mother' in human form." Another person, astonished at the care he saw lavished daily on the dying, could not stop himself from blurting out publicly, "I promised I would get that woman out of here, and I shall. But . . . I shall not get her out of this place before you get your mothers and sisters to do the work these nuns are doing."

In his book on Mother Teresa, Edward Le Joly tells another anecdote that he heard from Michael Gomes, whose family sheltered her in 1949. "One day, we saw alongside the Campbell Hospital . . . close to our house, a man dying on the road-side. Mother enquired; the hospital authorities could not accommodate him. We went to a chemist to get some medicine for him; when we returned with the medicines, the man was dead on the street. Mother did not hide her feelings.

Teresa is said to have once carried a dying woman in her arms through the streets, unable to find a hospital that would care for her. She does not wait for patients to come or be carried to her—instead she and the Missionaries go in search of the dying, who can still be seen on the streets of many cities, like the figures huddled beneath a truck here (opposite page). Another photograph (center left) shows Mother Teresa helping an elderly man along. Calcutta is said

'They look after a dog or a cat better than a fellow-man,' she said. 'They would not allow that to happen to their pets.' She went to the Commissioner of Police to complain about this state of affairs. That was the origin of the Kalighat Home for the Dying."

No matter what the origin, from then on every morning the police, accompanied by the sisters, carry to the Home for the Dying, right next to the residential neighborhood of Alipare,

to have 300,000 sidewalk dwellers, of whom about 1,000 die on the streets each month.

When no other transportation can be found, the Missionaries simply use their feet (above) and carry the destitute dying to the closest center where care can be found. Above all, they attempt to provide loving comfort and kindness—the medicine that can always help even when it is too late for anything else.

Here we see the Missionaries of Charity in their ceaseless efforts to gather up the homeless dying and bring them to a place where they can receive help, or at last die in peace surrounded by loving care.

Far left below: A rickshaw-type cart is one of many rudimentary vehicles that have been improvised and pressed into service by the Missionaries. The end justifies the means.

In Calcutta (left) the Missionaries have a motley fleet of cars, trucks, and buses to meet their various needs, including the collection of invalids. It is not unusual to see a dilapidated school bus like this one, painted blue and white, plying the city streets.

49

all those who cannot raise themselves from the gutter and who spend their dying breath in the most extreme state of neglect. They are gathered up regardless of their race or religion. It is hard to say how many there have been. Anywhere from thirty to sixty thousand. Mother Teresa is not the best bookkeeper in the world. But what difference do the numbers make? What is certain is that these people are cared for and loved. Once more they find a shred of human dignity and depart from this life with decency. "They lived like animals," says Mother. "At least they die like human beings." And she adds, "First of all we want to make them feel that they are wanted, we want them to know that there are people who really love them, who really want them, at least for the few hours that they have to live, to know human and divine love. That they too may know that they are the children of God, and that they are not forgotten and that they are loved and cared about and there are young lives ready to give themselves in their service."

As time went on, the work of gathering up the homeless dying was turned over to the Brothers, whom one could

expect to be more suited to the task than the diminutive Teresa and her nuns. Nevertheless the Home for the Dying Destitute remains very close to her heart. And the dying represent much more than a duty.

A girl came from outside India to join the Missionaries of Charity. We have a rule that the very next day new arrivals must go to the Home for the Dying. So I told this girl: "You saw Father during Holy Mass, with what love and care he touched Jesus in the Host. Do the same when you go to the Home for the Dying, because it is the same Jesus you will find there in the broken bodies of our poor." And they went. After three hours the newcomer came back and said to me with a big smile—I have never seen a smile quite like that—"Mother, I have been touching the body of Christ for three hours." And I said to her: "How—what did you do?" She replied: "When we arrived there, they brought a man who had fallen into a drain, and been

"They lived like animals. At least they die like human beings." At Nirmal Hriday, the Home for Dying Destitutes that Teresa founded in Calcutta, she is proud that no one dies uncared for or unloved. The hospital is staffed by one doctor, twenty sisters of the Missionaries of Charity, and various volunteers from both East and West. The first home for the dying, it was opened in 1952 and has a normal capacity of 110.

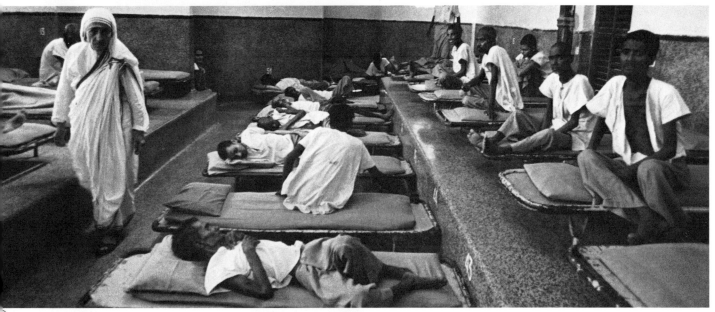

there for some time. He was covered with wounds and dirt and maggots, and I cleaned him and I knew I was touching the body of Christ."

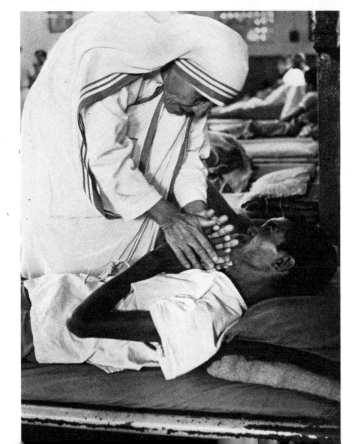

Inside what was once an elaborate building (opposite page), space is at a premium and conditions are primitive. Yet everyone who visits the place, filled with its poor incurables lying at close quarters on simple pallets (center above), is moved and touched by the surprising warmth and joy that pervade these rooms. What kind of strength does it take to fold the hands of a sick man as he breathes his last (left)? To the Missionaries, "these people are Christ."

51

FEEDING THE HUNGRY

From the beginning of her work among the poor, Mother Teresa has devoted herself to the constant task of feeding the hungry. In a country such as India, her efforts in this regard can be considered no more than a drop in the bucket: but the effort is made, the commitment exists, and the example stands for all to see and to imitate.

Many who have known and observed her, wonder how Mother Teresa has succeeded in feeding so many when supplies of basic necessities have often been scarce. One answer is that she has always shared whatever she and her helpers have had, be it ever so little. And another answer is found in a word she constantly uses: "Providence."

People have been prompt to compare her work with the "feeding of the five thousand" in the Gospel, and as is to be expected with someone like Teresa, a wealth of legends and "miracles" are already in circulation. Every time the larder has been bare, or when firewood was exhausted—or so we are told—Teresa or one of the other sisters would start to pray: and a visitor would promptly turn up bearing the needed sack of rice or the kindling.

Another tale, told in an Italian magazine, states that it suddenly started to rain in torrents one day immediately after Teresa had set out ninety-five cartons of powdered milk in the courtyard. The sisters' prayers did nothing to halt the downpour, which threatened to ruin all the milk powder. Teresa carried a large crucifix into the courtyard—in vain: the rain continued, for five days. The nuns were apparently unable to cover or move the precious milk.

But when the rain finally stopped, although many of the cartons were torn or perforated, not one container of milk powder—according to this story—was wet. The milk could be handed on to the needy.

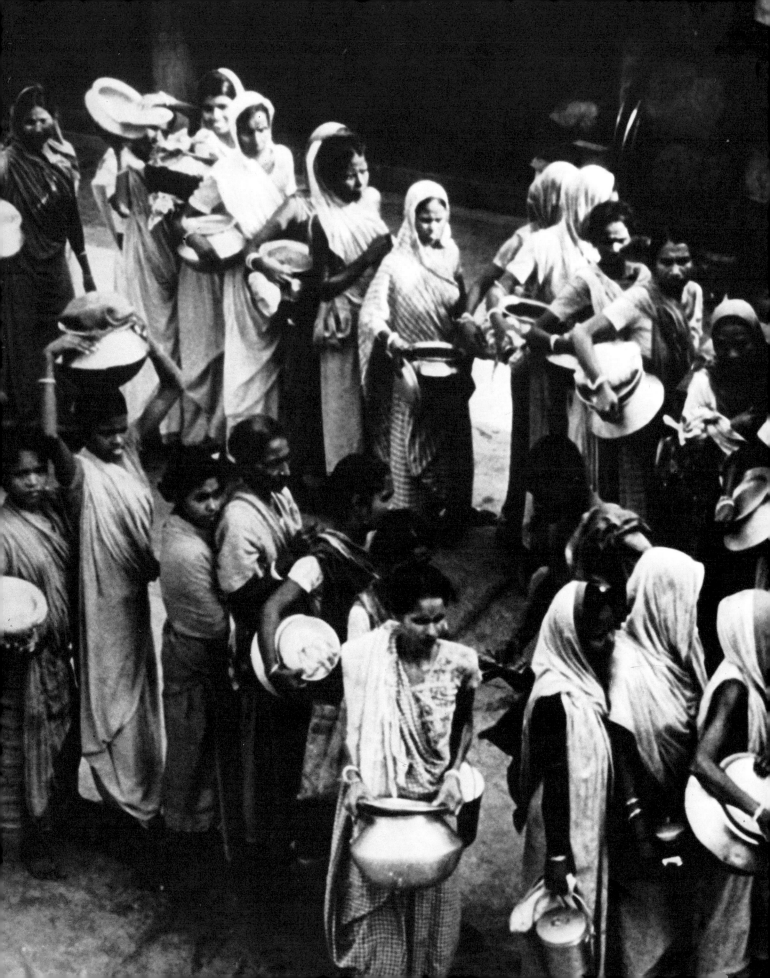

50,000 LEPERS

lepers as squatters on a tract of unused railroad property. The authorities have neither expelled the lepers nor given them official status: thus the buildings at Titagarh remain flimsy temporary structures that shake with each passing train. Some patients have even been hurt by coming too close to the rails. The Titagarh leper colony has prospered nevertheless, stretching out in both directions along the railroad tracks.

The lepers are treated medically—the majority are out-patients who come for brief treatment at irregular intervals—and also receive training so that they can make their own bandages and care for themselves as much as possible. Most members of the staff are lepers themselves, or arrested cases. The Missionaries hope to build Titagarh into a permanent colony for lepers and their families.

It is not easy to ensure that persons afflicted with leprosy

Then there are the lepers. Of some twenty million in the world, more than fifty thousand live in the region of Calcutta alone. It was in 1957 that Mother Teresa began to turn her attention to them. One day five lepers came to see her. They had been chased away from their work and no longer had shelter or food. That was no obstacle for Mother Teresa. Some benefactors furnished her with ambulances which she transformed into mobile clinics and on which she plows through the famous, leper-infested slums.

Today, thanks to new medicines, there has been success in checking this illness, which for centuries has been a shameful blight. "But," says Teresa, "when someone is undesirable, and there are no helping hands or loving hearts, then I don't think that this horrible illness can be cured." At Shantinagar—or City of Peace—on a thirty-four-acre plot given by the Indian government, she has built a rehabilitation center "so that," she says, "the cured lepers can learn a trade, and when they have returned home, they no longer have to beg."

Another of the Missionaries' important leper centers was founded some twenty-five years ago at Titagarh, an indus-trial town near Calcutta, where the nuns installed a group of

54

Progress has been made in treating leprosy since 1957, when Mother Teresa first became involved in work with the "unclean." She obtained an abandoned lot that ran along the railroad tracks at Titagarh, and organized a leper clinic there in huts that shook with each passing train. Now, at Shantinagar (below), the Missionaries have established clean, modern quarters where lepers are given medical treatment plus training so that they can support themselves instead of begging. The disease still afflicts some twenty million people throughout the world.

complete their cure. Sister Bernard, one of the Missionaries of Charity working at the Titagarh center, reports that as many as 5,000 persons are treated as out-patients at any one time. Each year brings about 1,000 new cases. Many are cured completely, but others interrupt their treatment. "You see," Sister Bernard told journalist Desmond Doig, "it's a long treatment and always there is the sad fact that poor lepers have nowhere to live. Their own people don't accept them." For one reason or another, these patients leave long gaps in the treatment, and meanwhile the disease worsens.

The disease is not only found among the poor. Indeed, it seems to afflict all economic levels and all age groups, even though poor sanitation conditions among deprived persons contribute to its spread. Many patients must come for treatment in secret. This may be one of the reasons why Mother Teresa so often repeats that the worst suffering is not to be wanted. Her attitude, which permeates all the Missionaries' clinics, is summed up in her words: "When I wash that leper's wounds, I feel I am nursing the Lord himself."

WHEREVER MOTHER TERESA APPEARS...

"The poor must know that we love them, that they are wanted. They themselves have nothing to give but love. We are concerned with how to get this message of love and compassion across."

To anyone who observes her at work it is obvious that she succeeds in communicating this message. Photographs capture something of her warmth and directness and concern, but when she approaches the people with whom she works, the people she has devoted her life to helping, the effect of her presence is almost palpable. From the responses one reads in these people's eyes, it is clear then that she reaches people and gives them something as important as food or shelter or medicine.

But what is extraordinary about Mother Teresa is not just her effect on those she wants to help. Even more remarkably, she has succeeded in inspiring and leading a whole army of followers, the thousands of members of the Missionaries of Charity throughout the world. She has seen that the work spreads far and wide, and that it will continue long after she is gone. What matters most to her, however, is that it be done with love, with care for each individual human being, and respect for the dignity and value that poverty, want, and illness cannot diminish.

And Jesus took a child,
and set him in the midst of them:
and when he had taken him in his arms,
he said unto them,
Whosoever shall receive
one of such children in my name, receiveth me:
and whosoever shall receive me,
receiveth not me, but him that sent me.

St. Mark 9:36–37

THE MISSIONARIES OF CHARITY

Little by little the young women joined her to help in her effort. The first ten were students who had been her pupils at Loreto. She had not forgotten that St. Joseph's feast day in 1949 when a young Bengali girl called and volunteered her services. This former student was to become her first nun, taking the name Sister Agnes, which is Teresa's baptised name. Soon she became the first mistress of the novices of the Congregation of the Missionaries of Charity and then Teresa's assistant. Teresa held out no illusions to any of these girls. "It will be a hard life," she told them. "Do you think you're up to it?" They arrived in a steady flow. Sister Frederick, Sister Gertrude, Sister Dorothy, Sister Marguerite . . .

This nucleus of the new congregation moved into a small house at 14 Creek Lane that had been put at their disposal. Here Teresa had her own room where she could stay up late answering mail from prospective members to her order without disturbing anyone else. She also began to draw up the Constitutions, otherwise known as the Rules of the Congregation. The other sisters were more or less camped together in another room. With the help of some benefactors, the bathrooms were installed. Well-to-do families sent her money that she had never even solicited. Obviously God was not abandoning her. She prayed and meditated, and she also taught her new recruits to care for the sick—the cancer-ridden, lepers, etc. And she taught them to speak tenderly to those who have nothing: "Let there be kindness in your face, in your eyes, in your smile, in the warmth of your greeting. For children, for the poor, for all those who suffer, and are alone, always have a cheerful smile. Don't only give your care, but give your heart as well." And she adds, "When you attend to the wounds and bruises of the poor, never forget that they are Christ's wounds." The misery surrounding them does not prevent this little community from living with a joy that is contagious. "Faith is prayer," Teresa tells her sisters. "It is strength, love. Joy is a net of love in which souls are captured. A heart burning with love is a joyous heart."

By the time she left Creek Lane, the number of nuns had grown to twenty-six. For the spiritual education of the novices, she called in several priests, but she herself took care of it on a daily basis, as she still does. Among other things, she

reminds them that they must maintain their love for the Eucharist, for their fellow-man, for prayer, for meditation, and above all for poverty—a harsh and Franciscan kind of poverty. It is not insignificant that the habit she chose is composed of a simple white sari with a crucifix clasped on the left shoulder. On their feet they wear simple sandals. And there is one more detail: each nun has the right to own three changes of clothing; one to be worn, while a second is being washed, and a third dried.

Returning then to October 1950: on the Feast of the Rosary, Pius XII transformed the little community into a diocesan congregation, that is, dependent on the local bishop. Fifteen years later, the pope raised it to the rank of Society of Pontifical Right, that is, under the direct control of Rome. To Teresa this was almost unimaginable, being aware as she was that many priests and nuns had dreamed of founding their own

orders only to be refused the authorization. Indeed, this was another miracle. From then on the recruits would be coming from everywhere—from India and from abroad. It was then that Teresa published the Constitutions of her congregation, which are the pivotal point of her work. The richness and balance in them admirably reflect the immense potential of kindness, charity, and devotion which are Teresa's natural endowments. Reading them, one can imagine the spiritual wealth on which she drew. Here one encounters the theology—although she would not like the word—philosophy, and mysticism of this woman, inspired at once by Ignatius of Loyola, Benedict, and Francis of Assisi. Mother Teresa is very much part of this extraordinary body of great founders of religious orders.

"Love and service are the key to giving." They are the secret of Teresa's work. Whoever has them can do anything. Nothing can resist these peaceful souls who have added to the three customary vows of poverty, chastity, and obedience a fourth: to consecrate their entire lives exclusively to the poorest of the poor without ever accepting any material recompense for their work.

In February 1952, having outgrown their headquarters, the missionaries moved to 54A Lower Circular Road in a three-story building. They were able to make this move thanks to money lent to them by the Archbishop of Calcutta: yet another considerable debt for this community which had already borrowed heavily, with faith as their only collateral. At first too large, the house quickly became almost too small.

Sister Frederick, the second of Teresa's volunteers, has been with her almost as long as Sister Agnes. She acts as Mother Teresa's representative on many occasions, as general secretary of the Missionaries of Charity, and is often spoken of as the likely successor of Teresa. Originally from Malta, Sister Frederick served for many years with the Missionaries in Rome. These two nuns have been joined by nearly 2,000 others; one class of novices and a nun working with refugees are seen below.

If the money was just trickling in, the volunteers came in a tidal wave. At the same time, Teresa was developing schools, dispensaries, and homes for the dying. Outside, word was getting around that a community of nuns was performing miracles. This word-of-mouth was enough to attract not

only curiosity but, more importantly, gifts, especially since the local press got involved. Someone asked these women how they could sacrifice themselves with such devotion. Teresa answered: "The poor are the gift of God. They are our love."

Little by little the congregation expanded all over India. India is a colossus of 620 million inhabitants, distributed in 21 states, where there are 14 official languages, not counting the 1,652 native tongues listed in the census. It is a formidable crossroads where Hindus (453 million), Muslims (72 million), Christians (17 million), Sikhs (12 million), and Buddhists intersect and intermingle. India became independent on 15 August 1947, while the Islamic state of Pakistan was formed at its borders and Calcutta was overrun with crowds of refugees. The nuns established themselves in Ranchi, Jhansi, Coimbatore, in the south, and in Mariapolli, Andhra Pradesh, a rural village that was certainly not lacking poor people. In Delhi, where the life expectancy for men did not exceed 19 years in 1911 and 52 years in 1974, Nehru came in person to open the children's home. Teresa likes to tell about this visit of the Indian Prime Minister.

"When the Prime Minister arrived, accompanied by Mr. Krishna Menon, I told them, 'Let's go first and greet the master of the house,' and I brought them to the chapel where I knelt to pray. Behind me Mr. Nehru bowed with his hands drawn. Mr. Krishna Menon mounted the altar to read an

61

inscription there and asked me what it meant. Then we went outside to be seated for the inaugural ceremony. Children brought a wreath for the Prime Minister and presented him with a spiritual bouquet. I explained to him that they had offered God prayers and small sacrifices in order to get these gifts for the Prime Minister. Then I asked him, 'Sir, do you want me to show you how we work?'

'No, Mother. It is not necessary. I know that already. That is why I have come here.'"

After Delhi, it was Bombay, another of India's important cities, in which Teresa established her sisters. After her arrival she created a minor scandal by declaring that the three- or four-story tenements in that city were worse than those of Calcutta. Nonetheless . . . It was in Bombay, during the International Eucharistic Congress of 1964, that the pope presented her with the convertible white Lincoln—a gift to him from an American—in which he had traveled through the streets of the capital of Maharashtra, lined with indescribably enthusiastic crowds. The raffle she held for this car was won by a non-Christian and brought her the tidy sum of a half-million rupees.

Invitations from bishops from all over the world were coming in asking her to set up establishments with them. Everyone had a claim on Teresa. In this year of grace, 1965, the pope declared the Missionaries a Society of Pontifical Right. It was the beginning of a new adventure.

Teresa's work has produced two other important offshoots, the Missionary Brothers of Charity and the Co-Workers.

The Brothers were at first a spontaneous formation, as candidates began to volunteer their services some twenty years ago. On 25 March 1963 the Archbishop of Calcutta gave his official blessing, once a sufficient number of candidates had been assembled and Rome had been petitioned for approval. Since that date, the male order has grown and prospered, though not at all to the same extent as the Sisters.

The Missionary Brothers of Charity, who now count a few hundred members, accomplish tasks as varied as those of the nuns. On these pages we see them engaged in medical work: the preparation of medicine in a leper dispensary (far left below), the heavy work of carrying stretchers, and (below) the care of the dying. The Brothers are charged with picking up the persons sick and dying in the streets, to bring them to the Missionaries' Home. In addition to this medical mission, the Brothers are also active as teachers and general helpers among the boys in the slums, and they themselves have built many of the facilities now used by the Missionaries of Charity. Though far fewer in number than the sisters, the Brothers too come from a great diversity of nations and backgrounds. Led by Brother Andrew, a former Jesuit with long service in Vietnam, the Brothers have their own chapter house in Calcutta, plus thirteen foundations in India and eight abroad. The work they must do has sometimes proved too much, and several postulants left the order.

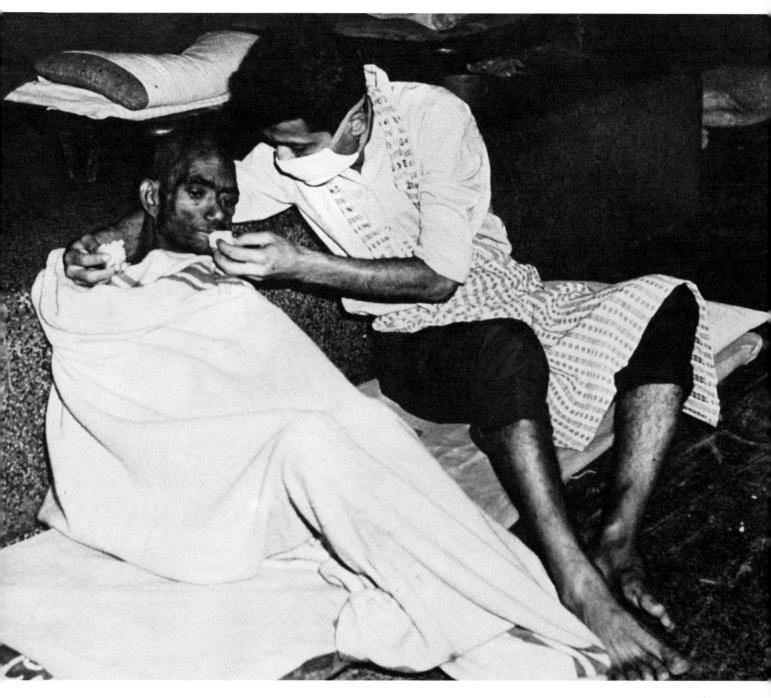

The other important helping arm is the group of co-workers who contribute so decisively to Mother Teresa's work. The International Association of Co-Workers of Mother Teresa was officially affiliated to the order of the Missionaries of Charity by Pope Paul VI, receiving his official blessing, on 26 March 1969. By that time, however, this ever growing group of supporters and fund-raisers had already completed a long unofficial history. It had begun modestly enough in 1954 with efforts by a group of volunteers to collect toys for Mother Teresa's annual Christmas party in Calcutta. Soon the volunteers were collecting money to purchase children's clothing, and the next step for the steadily expanding organization was to take over fund-raising for the work with lepers. Mrs. Ann Blaikie, chairman of the International Associa-

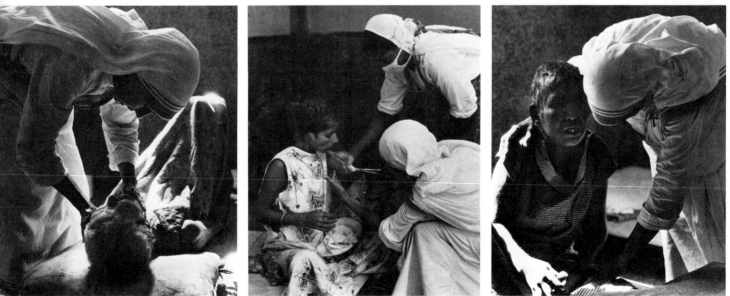

tion, has been instrumental in its work since the beginning and maintains a very successful close working relationship with Mother Teresa and the Missionaries. Today the Co-Workers have active, effective branches in more than twenty countries.

To aid further, Mother Teresa has organized a group of inva-lids whose prayer group, the Sick and Suffering, lends spiritual support to the Missionaries' efforts, and a group of contemplative monasteries throughout Europe which pray continually for the Missionaries. For Mother Teresa, these prayers are every bit as useful to her work as money, food, clothing, and medicine.

The life of the Missionaries of Charity is far from easy. It entails religious discipline, the triple vow of poverty, chastity, obedience, as well as constant proximity with pain and want and suffering. But above all this life is work. The hard work, beginning before dawn, will go on well after dark. A great deal of this physical labor is involved with cleanliness, the need to fight contagion and disease. In clinics that house lepers, beggars, and the dying, linen must be boiled (left), and the sick themselves (pictures below left) will have to be washed, treated, held, and comforted, not once but constantly. There are far more patients than helpers, and of course time, space, and supplies are also scarce.

A volunteer seeking to join the Missionaries must serve for six months as an aspirant, then for six months more as a postulant, before becoming a novice. The group of novices seen below are cleaning by hand the floor of the courtyard where so many persons gather each day for feeding and other activities.

THE WORK SPREADS ACROSS THE WORLD

The growth of the Missionaries of Charity and the Missionary Brothers, and the spreading of Teresa's work throughout the world, have proceeded at a phenomenal rate. The statistics listed here are impressive indeed, though of course they are incomplete. Incomplete first of all because it is nearly impossible to keep up with the Missionaries' growth, so that the figures we give here will be out of date before this book goes to print. But, even more to the point, statistics tell only one side of the story; to understand something, in human terms, about these remarkable people and their near-miraculous work it is necessary to listen to them. We have asked several of the Missionaries in diverse lands to describe their activities.

TONDO, PHILIPPINES: SISTER MARY TARCISIA, SUPERIOR

"We are happy to share with you this work of God—you on your part can help to make this love be known by all men.

"Our mission in Manila was established three years ago, when Mother Teresa arrived with three of our Sisters from India. This center operates today with eight professed Sisters and also from six to ten young Aspirants. Two years ago our second center in Manila was established here in Tondo. The Tondo center has the Home for the Destitute and the Dying, which consists of four pavillions for patients, whether young or old, who are unwanted, abandoned, neglected, and often in the terminal stages of very severe illnesses. Again, most of them are brought from streets and market places and squatter areas, where our Sisters find them and pick them up on their daily rounds to these places. In the 18 months of its existence this Tahanan has admitted over 230 patients, and out of these some 65 have died very beautifully, surrounded by the loving care and presence of our Sisters.

"The poor, the unwanted, the dying—for us they are Jesus. Because God cannot tell us a lie—and Jesus said: This is my body. Whatever you do to these least of my brethren, you do to Me. So we touch him twenty-four hours a day in his broken body, in his often terrible disguise....We touch him with our compassion.

"The poor are hungry not only for rice, but for God. And we bring them his Word, the Word of God."

BRONX, NEW YORK: SISTER PRISCILLA

"As for our mission here in New York, our Sisters came in 1971. It was the first convent Mother established here in the United States and remained the only one until June of last year, when two other houses came into being, in St. Louis, Missouri, and in Detroit, Michigan. When the Sisters arrived in New York with Mother, they took shelter with the Franciscan Sisters in Harlem, until the vacated convent of St. Rita's in the South Bronx was offered to us a few months later.

"Today, the Sisters go out to the elderly and the sick shut-ins and do for them whatever is needed in their homes. Many of them are fearful of going out into neighborhoods which have become unsafe over the years, and they virtually imprison themselves in apartments from which they cannot afford to move. Their world is small and when the Sisters come, they do not want them to leave. Each week we also visit hospitals and nursing homes for the chronically ill—many of whose patients receive fewer and fewer family visitors as their stay lengthens into years. On Saturdays and Sundays, we go to the men on Rikkers Island prison to say the Rosary and share Sunday Mass with them.

SEOUL

TOKYO

AIPEI

ANILA

DETROIT   NEW YORK

ST. LOUIS

LOS ANGELES
SANTA ANA

TOLUCA
MEXICO CITY   PORT-AU-PRINCE

GUATEMALA   CATIA LA MAR
SAN SALVADOR   CARACAS
PANAMA   CIUDAD GUAYANA

HANUBADE
TOKARARA   CHIMBOTE   BAHIA
KEREMA
PORT MORESBY   LIMA

KATHERINE

BOURKE   BUENOS AIRES
MELBOURNE

Starting alone in 1948, Teresa was soon joined by four nuns, and today the Missionaries of Charity have 250 sisters in Calcutta alone and 1,800 more located in congregations elsewhere in India and in 25 other countries. They operate 127 orphanages, 213 free dispensaries, 54 leprosariums, and 60 free schools. The Brothers have 13 congregations in India and eight more in as many countries.

Not included on the map are the many branch offices of the auxiliary organization, the International Co-Workers of Mother Teresa, which has centers in more than twenty countries.

Below: Port Moresby in Papua-New Guinea, *where Teresa founded a congregation in July 1974.*

"Early on we found that there were women—young and old, some ill of mind and others ill of body—who had no place to stay. We took them in and now have a larger building right behind our Convent to provide them with temporary shelter until we can have them relocated into some other more permanent living quarters. This same building serves as our kitchen; we serve a hot meal daily to sixty people.

"We have many children in our area too. And we prepare them for their First Holy Communion and for Confirmation. During the summer we bring them into our day care center so that they may be off the streets and less in danger of getting into trouble or being hurt.

"These are some of the needs of the people we try to meet and bring knowledge of God's ineffable love to them."

MISSIONARIES OF CHARITY

PORT-AU-PRINCE, HAITI: SISTER CARMELINE

"We came to Haiti in 1977. This is one of the poorest countries in the world. We were only three sisters in the beginning. Mother came with us. The first thing we did was to learn the language. One priest kindly helped us for two weeks to learn Creole and then we started to visit the poor people around us. And then we found out so many poor areas and also a place in the general hospital known as the 'depot'—where we found so many sick and abandoned people waiting to get a bed, but many die before entering inside. . . . Now we have a big home for the sick and dying. About sixty patients can be taken inside, and always it is full. Besides this we have a school for the slum children, right in the middle of one of the poorest areas. About two hundred slum children receive the education in our school. Then we have four dispensaries around Port-au-Prince.

"Then we have a nutrition center attended by four hundred children daily. God has blessed us a lot in this 2½ years. The need is so great—the poor are so good. We are so busy—no time to write a real letter."

ROTTERDAM, NETHERLANDS:
G. J. COLENBRANDER, NATIONAL LINK

"The Sisters in Rotterdam arrived in August 1977, found a little flat in a workman's area at the end of that year, and lived there to get acquainted with the people and the city during 1978. Working with demented old people, in the houses of the poor, lonely, and desparate. In the beginning there were four nuns and one aspirant, three Indians with Sister Monica in charge. The work has gradually grown and the sisters moved to a large house in the center of town (rather the rundown bit as was to be expected). There they can give shelter to about six to eight persons for the night. People who can't find anywhere else to lay their heads to rest, for whatever reason. A lot of them colored. Somehow not yet integrated into Dutch society. The sisters live according to the rules of their orders. Real contemplatives in the world. They get up at five, meditate and pray, then mass and then out to work. Back home for prayer and dinner and so on. On Saturday afternoons the house is open for prayer meetings for all who care to come. The atmosphere in the house is happy and peaceful. It is an uphill struggle for them as the poverty of Holland is more in the spirit than in the body, as you will imagine."

GAZA, ISRAEL: SISTER MARY ALOYSIUS

"As Missionaries of Charity we take a vow to give wholehearted free service to the poorest of the poor. Here in Gaza, we gather the poor children and teach them to be clean, not to be selfish, and some counting etc., like a nursery school. We find that this is very helpful for the children as they come from poor living conditions.

"We distribute flour, soya, bulgar, milk, and rice to the old

Scenes from two recently founded congregations (below). A group of elderly persons pose with the Missionaries in the second center in Rome, at Trastevere (founded 1977). The second photograph shows young volunteers from Minnesota who went to Haiti in the winter of 1980 to help build a clinic and school. In 1979 a total of twelve new congregations were founded, including for the first time a center in a Communist country, at Zagreb, Yugoslavia.

ladies and women with small children. We also receive medicines which we distribute at that time. We go to the homes to pray the Rosary every Saturday and also visit the families and teach Catechism in a simple way to the children."

PORT LOUIS, MAURITIUS: SISTER MARY ALEXANDRA

"While we were studing the language of the people, we started to visit the families, and found they are from different origins, Africans, Indians, Chinese, French etc. While visiting the families we felt the need of the medical work and began a dispensary in the open air. Sister Rikta who was also a nurse did the consultation. The Ministry of Health supplied us with some medicines whenever we needed. In December 1972, Sister Tarcisia started a commercial class for the young girls who have finished their school final and are waiting for a job. It was very helpful for them since, in every work, they asked for a typist. Today many of our students are working as secretaries in the offices. In the meantime we were also preparing some craft hand works to get some girls for the sewing class.

"On 26 August 1973, we had the visit of our dearest Mother (Mother M. Teresa) in Mauritius, to which we were eagerly looking forward since our foundation in Mauritius. During an interview with the MBC on TV Mother explained about our work and invited the people who are interested to form a group of 'Co-Workers of Mother Teresa' to help us with the work as they do all over the world. Many have responded and are doing fine works. Now we have over fifty Co-Workers.

"May the Lord bring more fervent laborers to His harvest which is plentiful and ripe."

*We must be able to radiate the joy of Christ, express it in
our actions. If our actions are just useful actions that give
no joy to the people, our poor people would never be able
to rise up to the call which we want them to hear,
the call to come closer to God. We want to make them feel
that they are loved. If we went to them with a sad face,
we would only make them much more depressed.*

TERESA: A PORTRAIT

Mother Teresa, or just "Mother", as she is known to her friends the poor, is a name and a face. Today everyone knows her. The media have made it their business to make her a star. But how could anyone accuse her of vanity? The gilded halls of royal palaces, whether English or Scandinavian, are only places to receive a prize for the use of the destitute. They are not her cup of tea. In fact, she is wary of these places and wastes no time in them. Luxury frightens her, and she avoids it studiously. She is as comfortable with it as a tramp in a plush apartment. She is a humble nun, who seeks only to hide behind the veil, to disappear into anonymity, to accomplish modest tasks modestly; something few people in our competitive consumer society consider a duty, much less an honor.

Like all "stars," she has been launched by television and magazines into the constellation of Important People, into the forefront of the news, for one brief hour, before, like the others, she gets back to serious work.

It is only right that charity—a synonym for love—should have its own stars, just as in show business, industry, and politics. Not that Teresa is a normal superstar, by any means. Refusing fame in her own right, she constantly reminds us of those she represents: the hungry and disinherited. It is they who brought her to our attention, and now she refuses to let them be forgotten by a selfish world. Isn't it true that without this refuse of humanity, no one would have spoken of Mother Teresa? That would have been all right with her. As she

never tires of pointing out, "Only a lack of love is responsible for poverty in the world." It is a problem that cannot be ignored.

This lack of love is a sin, a waste. It is a mortal sin, which she and her sisters have long been striving with all their might to redress through their own self-sacrifice. "And what of it?" she exclaimed one day. "There are those who take better care of their dogs and cats than their human brothers." It is a bitter and plain testimony. Mother Teresa's accusations are without rancor, but equally without pity.

She might have done something other than use her life for the downtrodden. She could have led a contemplative life, in the shadow of a cloister, swallowed up in meditation and above all in prayer, which is as indispensable to her as the light of day. "Prayer," she says, "enlarges the heart." She might have been a singer. She is said to have had a beautiful soprano voice. As a young girl she was an enthusiastic chorister and loved to lead the way in song, accompanying herself on the accordion or mandolin, while on outings with her family or friends. Having decided to answer God's calling at any cost, she might at least have continued in this course, as a private-school nun teaching geography to India's jet set—who certainly have as much right as any others to be evangelized.

Indeed, the young Gonxha might have done many things, for her mother, despite their limited means after the father's death, brought her up well and taught her to live strictly. Her mother even sent her through secondary school (which was rare for girls at the time), though without any grand culture. She had something loftier than culture: a great heart. She was raised in a religion that was somewhat Jansenist, strict and old-fashioned, which some have gone so far as to dismiss as sanctimonious. One could call it a simple faith, but after all, grace takes many forms.

"Work never distracted me from God," she likes to repeat. And however exalting that work might be, it is also exhausting and enervating. So much so that her fellow nuns candidly admit that they live in a state of perpetual fatigue. And so does Teresa, according to all evidence, and to judge from this confession made one day when she was more tired than usual: "At times I feel like an empty vessel, a limp rag. I feel so

alone, so miserable." Even she knows moments when it seems she cannot go on any longer.

She is indeed an odd woman whose match is rarely, if at all, to be met with nowadays. The strength of her spirit awakens the dynamism dormant in the most lethargic souls, heats up even a lukewarm conscience, spurs on the faint-hearted. Who can—who dares—resist her? Her charisma is such that she acts as a kind of detonator unleashing a tidal wave of activity, like St. Paul, Francis of Assisi, or Vincent de Paul and other saints before her—all great beacons of humanity, and all obsessed by the Gospel.

This frail angel need only appear, armed with nothing but a rosary, for the world to be set ablaze. She is only a little wisp of a woman—barely five feet tall—her white sari of coarse cloth hanging limply on her frame. Her accent in English is as rough as her native Yugoslav mountains, her back stooped over with age, her face sun-baked like a Roman tile, her hands sturdy and rugged like those of the peasants of her native Macedonia. And yet those same hands are so gentle with the dying, with the lepers, and with children who search for any shred of tenderness. Even if she appears delicate, she has a force of nature which will not stop until the final hour. She is always ready for combat, to charge like a bulldozer, to move mountains in the name of a God to whom she has dedicated her life, in the name also of the humble of the human species. She would fain retreat behind these souls, to become anonymous: "It is not I who count," she told a curious journalist. "I am not important." It is as if she needed to be excused for talking about herself too much.

So much is she identified with the poor, that she has ended up living like them and resembling them. All she owns is a sari edged in blue and a bucket for washing herself; her sole shelter is a cell, whose doors are always open. Furnished like a monk's cell, it has a small bed and a simple wooden table where piles of mail are heaped. She stays up until one a.m. answering this correspondence, usually by hand. Meanwhile the other sisters sleep three or four to a room, and as if this tiny space were already too much for them, they keep moving their lodgings. There are no comforts in Mother Teresa's order. There is not even a fan, which would certainly be wel-

71

"Where there is mystery, there must be faith. Faith, you cannot change no matter how you look at it. Either you have it, or you don't. For us, it is very simple because our feet are on the ground. We have more of the living reality. There was a time when the Church had to show majesty and greatness. But today, people have found that it does not pay. They have found the emptiness of all that pomp so they are coming down more to the ground, and in coming down there is the danger that they are not finding their proper place.

come in a summer heat that can reach 113 °F. "How can I face the poor?" she says. "How can I tell them, 'I love you and understand you,' if I don't live like them?" That is really the secret of this woman, to whom—as even she recognizes—God has made the superb gift of good health.

Despite this she is by no means a stranger to what St. John of the Cross called "the dark night"—those empty hours which she quickly overcomes because there is no time to lose, and because there are people everywhere who are crying, suffering, waiting for her, counting on her, looking to her for a miracle. One wonders if she has ever been tempted to abandon it all. To entertain such an idea would not even be insulting to her. Perhaps it was with this in mind that she reported an anecdote from the life of the famous Benedictine monk Dom Marmion. Tempted for an instant to quit his order, he called out from a prostrate position in front of the tabernacle, "May I be cut into pieces rather than quit the monastery." And Teresa adds, "Are we strong enough to prefer being torn apart to abandoning Christ? Changing professions is not like changing clothes. Nowadays everything is slackening. Let us cling to the rock which is Christ."

There may be mistakes, many mistakes. We may make mistakes. But He cannot make mistakes. He will draw the good out of you. That's the beautiful part of God, eh? That He can stoop down and make you feel that He depends on you. The same thing with Our Lady, no?

When the angel was sent to Her and said, "You are to be the Mother of Jesus," Our Lady emptied Herself and said, "Do unto me according to Thy will. I am the handmaid of the Lord."

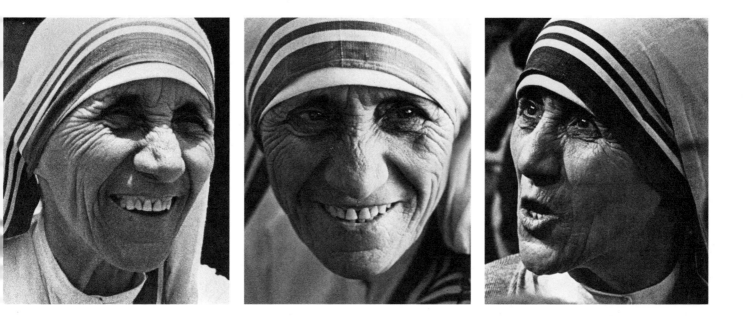

When all is said and done, the poor are her true passion and her only family. Her veneration and respect for this family is so great that she is able to declare, "The greatest injustice against the poor is to deprive them of their dignity. These are really noble people. We can easily do without a meal once in a while. But they—they are hungry day after day, and die abandoned. Day after day, thrown into the streets without a roof over their heads, they wander. Day after day they struggle to survive, and it is this struggle that takes such immense courage, that makes their nobility."

These are not hollow words. Mother Teresa knows what she is saying. It is not enough to give alms to these ragged and starving vagabonds. That would be too simple. It would be getting off too easily. It is true: they have their dignity, and misfortune itself is their nobility. In the Beatitudes, the Gospel expresses the same thought in different terms, in immortal words: "Blessed are the poor.... Blessed are they that mourn.... Blessed are they which do hunger and thirst after righteousness." These words have not always fallen on deaf ears. Occasionally there have been some who have taken heed. Some, like Mother Teresa.

That this magnetic woman has been filled with the spririt of God, is borne out in this impressive anecdote reported in the first book written about her. It occurred during the shooting of a film on the renowned Home for the Dying Destitute of Calcutta. The room was so dark that the cameraman thought he would have to give up filming. Finally they shot some footage anyway. Imagine the astonishment of the technicians when, on developing the film, they saw the Home for the Dying bathed in a soft, but nonetheless superb, light. "I myself," Malcolm Muggeridge wrote, "am absolutely convinced that the technically unaccountable light is, in fact, the Kindly Light Newman refers to in his well-known exquisite hymn.... Mother Teresa's Home for the Dying is overflowing with love, as one senses immediately on entering it. This love is luminous like the haloes artists have seen and made visible round the heads of saints. I find it not at all surprising that the luminosity should register on a photographic film." The same journalist also reports that when the film was broadcast on British television, the public responded with an outpouring of letters, telling how personally touched they were by this woman.

73

Her love of children is manifested in many of her activities, as well as in her unflinching opposition to abortion—a subject she does not hesitate to raise even in a Nobel Prize speech, much less in overpopulated India. She has a fine rapport with children and can reach even the most difficult disturbed youngsters.

Left: She is fully at home now in India, her adopted home. "I'm an Indian, I don't even remember for how many years now." She received Indian citizenship in 1948.

A personality with the dimensions of Mother Teresa is bound to become a legend, like St. Francis whose "little flowers" have become world famous throughout the centuries. The best of her legends—a true story in fact— is that one day Mother Teresa was unable to pay for a trip and offered her services as a stewardess. Since then Indira Gandhi has put an end to such difficulties by giving her a free pass on the railroads and Indian airlines.

Of course no one attributes miracles to her as yet. That will come, and more. This is not to say that stories, and extraordinary ones at that, are not already circulating. Take this one, for example. In 1973 a private society gave her the gift of a large modern building surrounded by a plot of land. She baptised it "gift of Love," and filled it with sick people, including the mentally ill. During a visit to a ward for these patients, one of the young girls there was becoming very agitated in her barricaded section of the room. When she saw the visitors, she was suddenly seized with such a violent fit that she climbed up on her bed and started to knock against the window with enough force to break the glass. Mother Teresa went to speak to her and clasped her firmly in her arms, all the while addressing her with reassuring words. Everyone held his breath expecting the worst. In the end, nothing happened, and the girl was pacified.

Poverty is the creation of you and me, a result of our refusal to share with others. God did not create poverty, He created only us. The problem will not go until we are able to give up greed. I think there is no place in the world which is free from poverty and injustice, not even the socialist countries. I'm a missionary, and it's divine providence that guides the missionaries from place to place. But I'm an Indian, I don't even remember for how many years now.

India is my country. In giving me the Nobel Award, the world has acknowledged the work of love and peace. Gandhi had said something so beautiful, "He who serves the poor, serves God."

When it comes to making the most of supplies and provisions, Mother Teresa (though she believes in Providence) proves to be canny, shrewd, punctilious, and resourceful. Here she is seen supervising a delivery of materials. She herself used to ride on the carts that were piled high with rice for the poor, to prevent loss, damage, and pilferage. When Pope Paul gave her a white 1964 Lincoln automobile, she organized a raffle which netted five times the car's selling price.

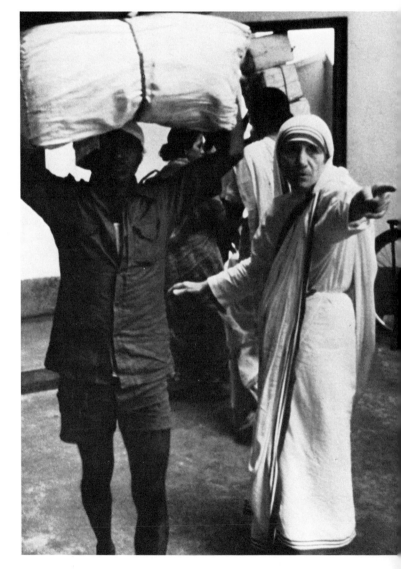

Again, the story is told that once a bull was let loose in a road where a crowd of lepers were gathered. One old man had already been thrown down and wounded, when suddenly Teresa came and put herself in the path of the beast. Opening her arms, she succeeded in calming the bull, which retreated without further ceremony. These are charming stories, if perhaps embellished. And even if they are, why shouldn't we believe those who report them so piously?

She speaks in parables, such as: "I can give fish to the poor but not the line for fishing." These would be obscure words if she herself did not provide the key. "A sick person," she explains, "hasn't the strength to cast the line or the net. Our task is to pull in the line. When it is done, it is up to you who have the means and the strength to teach them to fish, to provide the line and net. That is how sharing begins."

Mother Teresa has her principles, and as noted before, she has learned these principles at her mother's knee. It is difficult to reproach her for them, even if she irritates certain people with her insistant prayers to the Sacred Heart and the Virgin. In the name of principles stemming from her childhood, she proves to be intransigent. For instance, her stand on contraception and abortion might shock some persons, considering her experience in underdeveloped countries and above all in India, where the galloping population has caused the adop-

tion of laws to deal with the problem. To those countries—rich or poor—where such legislation exists, she vents her anger, and challenges them to have courage and hope instead. "We must pray for them, because it is a great sin. If abortions are permitted in the richest countries, which know no want, they are for me the poorest of the poor. Our little children are rejected and unloved. Today the problem worrying so many people is not only that the world is overpopulated, but that this supposedly proves that Providence cannot provide for her own newborn babies.... I would like to open up many institutions for children in those countries. We have some small ones in India, and so far we have not had to refuse a single child. And what is even more marvelous, God provided each child, who might otherwise have died at the hands of his own parents, with a home and new parents.... For us in India, this is a marvelous thing, because, according to the law, these children are untouchables.... Life belongs to God, and we haven't the right to destroy it." In the name of these same principles, she warns against the upsets in the Church ever since Vatican Council II. "The Church wants a renewal, but that does not mean a change of habits. A renewal must remain faithful to the spirit of the letter." And again she says, "These are difficult times for the Church. Don't worry about the gossip though. You hear about priests and nuns renouncing their orders and about broken homes. But don't forget that there are thousands and thousands of priests and nuns and faithful families. This trial will purify the Church of human infirmities, and it will emerge more beautiful and true." This strength and courage to confront received ideas are derived from her faith. "Nobody," she says, "can take that from me. If, in order to radiate the love of Christ among the unfortunate, there is no alternative but to stay in India, I will stay there; but I will not renounce my faith. I am prepared to give up my life, but not my faith."

This faith is expressed in all sorts of ways. But it is above all nourished by the Eucharist. For Teresa the "real presence" is never in doubt, and that certain priests would question this dogma is scandalous to her. Another rather harmless but significant detail: she cannot understand why those same priests don't genuflect before the Holy Sacrament. Once when a clergyman attacked the dogma of the Eucharist in front of her nuns, she simply asked him never to set foot again in her convent.

It is hard to imagine the importance prayer has in her life. "The soul of prayer," she confides, "is a soul of profound silence.... We must get accustomed to the silence of the spirit, eyes, and tongue.... We need to find God, and he cannot be found in noise and restlessness. God is the friend of silence. See how nature—trees, flowers, grass—grow in silence.... All our words will be useless unless they come from within—words which do not give the light of Christ increase the darkness."

To her nuns she once wrote, "Be circumspect with your words. Emulate the discretion of the Virgin. She didn't breathe a word to Joseph of the Angel's message, but kept it in her heart and let God intervene. Excell in obedience.... Don't be blind.... What is a Saint if not a resolute soul, a soul which uses strength to act? To be resolved to be a Saint costs a lot... I want to be a Saint who is put here to say, I will divest myself of everything that is not God." Another time she said to her nuns, "When you go to Heaven, our Lord won't ask, 'Was your Superior intelligent, understanding, cheerful?' He is only going to ask one thing: 'Did you obey me?'"

And another time: "My children, what are these drops of oil in our lamps? They are the little things of our everyday life: faithfulness, punctuality, little words of good will, simply a word for others; our way of being quiet, of looking, speaking, and acting."

It is first and last for the poor, "her poor," that this flame burns; for they are, she says, the gift of God, hope. She can wax eloquent on the subject of the poor: "The greatest sin is the absence of love and charity, the terrible indifference to our fellow man who, lying in the gutter, is exposed to exploitation, corruption, indigence, and disease.... If sometimes our poor people have had to die of starvation, it is not because God didn't care for them, but because you and I didn't give, were not instruments of love in the hands of God; because we did not recognize him, when once more Christ came in distressing disguise—in the hungry man, in the lonely man, in the homeless child, and seeking for shelter."

One Christmas Teresa went to see her lepers. She told them that they are the gift of God, that He loves them with a special love, and that their misfortune is no sin. At this point an old man, completely disfigured by the disease, interrupted: "Mother, would you tell me that again, because I've always heard that no one loves us. It is wonderful to know that God

*Thoughtfulness is the beginning of great sanctity.
Our vocation, to be beautiful, must be full of thought for
others. Jesus went about doing good. Our Lady in Cana
only thought of the needs of others and made their needs
known to Jesus.*

loves us. Say it again." She tells the story that once a wounded man refused to give her the name of his assailant. When she insisted, he finally responded, "His suffering will not lessen my suffering." All of these stories go to show that the most destitute have something to teach us. Another time she entrusted an abandoned child to one of her sisters with instructions to do nothing but play with him. "And," she says, "his appetite came back." This is another "little flower." To speak in public is a real trial for her. "For me it is more difficult than taking care of a leper." She looks over the heads of the audience and charges ahead. She says, "Don't look for spectacular actions. What is important is the gift of yourselves. It is the degree of love that you invest in each of your deeds." She adds, "I believe the people of today do not think that the poor are like them as human beings. They look down on them. In fact, the poor have as much right to the things of life and of love as anybody else."

She admits, "I do not agree with the big way of doing things. To us what matters is an individual. . . . If we wait till we get the numbers, then we will be lost in the numbers. . . . Love is a fruit which is always in season."

All this by no means prevents her from speaking her mind, even to crowned heads. Even on receiving the Templeton Award from Prince Philip of Edinburgh, she did not mince her words: "Let us thank God," she said, "that Mr. Templeton has had the courage to give, for the glory of God, the capital that Providence has so generously given him. . . .

"In England and other places, in Calcutta, in Melbourne, in New York, we find lonely people who are known by the number of their room. . . . Do we really know that there are some people, maybe next-door to us? Maybe there is a blind man who would be happy if you would read the newspaper for him; maybe there is a rich person who has no one to visit him—he has plenty of other things, he is nearly drowned in them, but there is not that touch and he needs your touch. Some time back a very rich man came to our place, and he said to me: 'Please, either you or somebody, come to my house. I am nearly half-blind and my wife is nearly mental; our children have all gone abroad, and we are dying of loneliness, we are longing to hear a human voice.'"

You should spend at least half an hour in the morning, and an hour at night in prayer. You can pray while you work. Work doesn't stop prayer, and prayer doesn't stop work. It requires only that small raising of mind to Him. "I love you, God, I trust you, I believe in you, I need you now." Small things like that. They are wonderful prayers.

Once in Melbourne, Mother Teresa visited an old man whom everyone else had passed by. His room was in a horrible state and she wanted to clean it up. After protesting for some time, he finally consented. In this room there was a splendid lamp covered with dust. The following dialogue ensued: "Why don't you turn the lamp on?" asked the nun. "For whom?" answered the man. "No one comes to see me. I don't need the lamp."

"And if the sisters come to see you, will you turn the lamp on?"

"Yes, if I hear a human voice."

Some time later the old man sent her this message: "Tell my friend that the lamp she lighted in my life is still burning."

Perhaps these are just trivial anecdotes or whims. To accommodate the whims of the poor, Teresa would answer, is to see each man in his own right, to take his hand so that he knows he is being looked after, considered, and needed. We never know how much a smile can accomplish. And she gives this advice: "Let no one ever come to you without leaving better and happier. Be the living expression of God's kindness; kindness in your face, kindness in your eyes, kindness in your smile. In the slums we are the light of God's kindness to the poor.... Thoughtfulness is the beginning of great sanctity. Our vocation, to be beautiful, must be full of thought for others. Jesus went about doing good. Our Lady in Cana only thought of the needs of others and made their needs known to Jesus."

Providence has made Mother Teresa an impressive and charismatic gift: imagination. She never runs out of ideas for solving the most complicated problems. Whether in Yemen, Addis-Ababa, Lima, Gaza, Schivpur, Rome, Belfast, Harlem, or Bangladesh, she is everywhere at once; in the midst of lepers, cholera victims, and the dying. With Cambodian refugees, Jews, and Arabs. She is only sorry that the rich, who would like to share the misfortune of others occasionally, and in their fashion, "don't give until it hurts."

Mother Teresa concerns herself with the needs of others to the smallest detail. Once, in a hovel, she found an abandoned family: six children, cared for by their eldest sister, a girl of fourteen. The father had disappeared, their mother was dead.

Mother Teresa took the family on, but did not have the courage to separate the children, who insisted on staying together. Having succeeded in raising a sum of 7,000 rupees, she decided on her own authority to put aside 5,000 as a dowry for the eldest daughter. Several years later, thanks to the money, the girl was able to marry without any problem. Nonetheless, people criticized Mother Teresa for putting aside for later this money that could have been spent to better purpose. This is not the only time that she has helped a young girl to get together a trousseau.

Teresa has truly earned the name "Mother."

Such is Sister Teresa: a simple soul, a pure spirit of staggering dynamism, always ready to fly to the aid of whoever calls; a woman of strict piety, whose integrity resembles the spirit of childhood embodied by the Gospels; a flame perpetually burning. A phenomenon of nature, undoubtedly. A poor one among the poor. Their advocate. Their servant. A refuge for all the abandoned of the earth. A hope, and hopefulness itself. All of God's tenderness is met with in her.

A revealing picture of Mother Teresa during a visit to Freiburg, Germany, 1978. Her religious belief, like the religious order she directs, is founded on asceticism. Whether it is a question of rising to attend Mass at five in the morning, or cleaning and tending the filthy and diseased, or fasting or doing without sleep, or just kneeling on a hard floor when no cushion is available—Teresa's faith seems to allow her, or even oblige her, to do the things that most persons would refuse to consider.

TERESA IN THE WIDE WORLD

Teresa has seen them all—kings, princes, dukes, heads of state, ministers, cardinals, and the Pope himself. She uses all the greats of the world as a means to carry out her mission and to defend the liberty of the poor. Money has no odor, as the saying goes. She accepts the gifts given to her as a due.

The powerful have never intimidated her. For them Teresa has the royal majesty of one in whom God dwells. It is she, rather, who awes them. As a poor person she is free. She makes no demands either in her own name or for herself. Indeed it is the important people of the world who have an eternal debt to those whom life has rejected. For kings and princes Teresa is a living reproach and, perhaps, their good conscience, an authentic testimony to the Gospel.

In 1976 Prime Minister Indira Gandhi of India presented Mother Teresa with an Honorary Doctorate from the Santiniketan Visva-Bharati University, placing the university scarf over her shoulders. By then Teresa was already something of a celebrity.

MEDIA STAR, MEDIA SAINT

For some twenty years Mother Teresa went about her work without attracting particular attention outside India. Desmond Doig, a journalist on India's major newspaper, *The Statesman,* had been writing about her inside the country almost since the beginning, but did not produce his well-known book on Mother Teresa until 1976. The International Association of Co-Workers, though their efforts began as early as 1954, worked behind the scenes in relative quiet and were not officially linked to the Missionaries until 1969. It was about this time—and perhaps partly due to the Co-Workers in England—that the world began to sit up and take notice and the insatiable appetite for information about Mother Teresa began to make itself felt.

One of the first decisive events in this media career was a BBC television program taped in 1967, in which Teresa was interviewed, during a visit to England, by author Malcolm Muggeridge. The producers decided the tape was dull and disap-

pointing, "barely usable" except perhaps in a late-night program. When it was finally shown on a Sunday evening, as Muggeridge later wrote, "The response was greater than I have known to any comparable program, both in mail and in contributions of money for Mother Teresa's work.... [Letters] came from young and old, rich and poor, educated and uneducated: all sorts and conditions of people. All of them said approximately the same thing—this woman spoke to me as no one ever has, and I feel I must help her."

84

This program, and the recognition that came from the growing number of international awards she was winning, set off something of a furor, which has still not abated. Books, interviews, filmed TV reports, leaflets, photographs, personal appearances—all the apparatus of stardom was brought to bear, with one enormous difference: the star, a nun, refusing to accept notice in her own right, constantly sought to draw attention to the sufferers of the world. Her motto: "I am not important."

The press, the world over, has been unanimous in its praise. Even *Time* magazine, while reporting some criticism of Mother Teresa's stand on abortion, still referred to her in its 1975 cover article as "a living saint."

Seldom has a public figure been heralded in such unanimously approving terms. For the past five years the pitch has been steadily raised. If she was a "living saint" to *Time*, the Italian, French, and German press went farther yet: for them Teresa was "an angel." The high point of all this glory seems to have come in the year of Teresa's Nobel Peace Prize award, when no praise seemed high enough and no newspaper failed to compete.

"Mother Teresa's unique claim to our admiration and affection," wrote *The Guardian* of London on learning she was to receive the Nobel Prize, "is that for nearly thirty years she has made a hell on earth a somewhat more endurable place in which to live and die for God knows how many thousands—possibly millions by now." Hamburg's influential *Die Welt* also sang her praises: "She is not political, she believes in God and tries to help those who are in a miserable condition." The *Verdens Gang* of Oslo called her "a woman who has during her whole life worked to help others, to relieve want and pain, to give respect and understanding to all people irrespective of their social status."

It was far from unusual at that time to see normally reserved, even cynical newspapers waxing lyrical, indeed a bit sentimental, on the subject of the Nobel winner. *The Washington Post,* the paper whose tough investigative reporting had first unearthed the Nixon Watergate scandal, spoke of Teresa as "a symbol of total charity and selflessness" and—in what was now a near obligatory refrain—"a living saint."

PUBLICITY

I have to go to Santiniketan to receive a degree. I don't know why universities and colleges are conferring titles upon me. I never know whether I should accept or not; it means nothing to me. But it gives me a chance to speak of Christ to people who otherwise may not hear of him.

In the last ten years Teresa has had to face a new range of duties: administration of her order of some 2,000 nuns and brothers throughout the world, liaison with the International Co-Workers of Mother Teresa (with branches in more than 20 countries), public speeches and receptions (opposite page) as well as contact with the rich and famous. She is seen above with U. S. Senator Edward Kennedy and a reporter. When the "Nobel fever" became too much, she retired from all press visits and interviews and was available only to the poor.

"If you are humble, nothing will bother you, neither praise nor slander, because you know what you are."

Teresa does not concern herself much with praise. She does not claim any special merits for herself. Her faith in God eclipses everything. As a schoolgirl she learned that humility is a virtue. "I feel like a pencil in God's hand," she once said. And as the poet Paul Claudel tells us, "God writes straight with curved lines." To be able to read between the lines, to find the goal through a labyrinthine course, is much easier said than done.

Thus it was despite herself, and certainly not for herself, that Mother Teresa became ensnared in the net of publicity. Without the media her name might never have become known in India. Even though it is well-known—a fact Teresa repeats constantly—that sanctity is never acquired, but is rather an aspiration and a desire, the battle to achieve it goes on daily, continuously. For months and months Teresa's fame spread across oceans. People were talking about her everywhere. Her poor, the terminally ill in her Home for the Dying filled columns in the newspapers. People were touched and moved and sometimes even became conscious of the reality of poverty.

Teresa accommodated such publicity all the more willingly because she had no other means to solicit contributions, medicine, vitamins, antibiotics, and above all soap which she needs so badly for her poor. And then, she says, perhaps new vocations will result. It is decidedly true: God writes straight with curved lines. The Nobel Prize was only the outcome of all those flashbulbs going off in the face of a humble nun who was obviously irritated by the publicity. She had from the beginning devoted herself to a life in the shadows, to meditation, and to the poor. In the last analysis, she contents herself with the knowledge that it is through this "personality" that the poor themselves have become celebrated. It is a fair resolution of the problem.

To get her to talk about herself, one practically has to force her by convincing her that it is the poor who benefit from her image. This is one way among others that she shows her acceptance of the exigencies of the modern world.

Never has publicity affected her humility. In 1950 Cardinal Spellman wanted to write her biography. Teresa refused. "My life or yours, it's still just a life," she answered the prelate.

It is her particular habit always to preach the Gospel. If St. Paul were to return to earth, it is said, he would use television and the media. Because of the swiftness of communication it is possible to know instantly what is happening from one end of the earth to the other. Today, amid all the images of war, violence, worldliness appears this smiling face, her eyes filled with the fire of religious fervor. That image says everything; it is like a flash of light, an illumination. God does indeed write straight with curved lines. Teresa, the great master builder, is the proof. She speaks in the name of all the poor, for Christ and for the outcast.

"Let's not have a cult of the personality.
It is He who has done everything. It has all been His work."

A peripatetic Mother Teresa has visited all the congregations of her Missionaries throughout the world and is repeatedly called to Rome and to the major capitals to receive prizes or attend religious conferences. She manages to obtain free passage, thus sparing the Missionaries a financial burden. Here we see her (from left to right) arriving in Vancouver for the 1976 Habitat Conference, in Frankfurt holding flowers, in Philadelphia for the 1976 Eucharistic Conference, airborne in prayer (opposite page), and finally back in Calcutta with "her" children, who are never forgotten, no matter where she goes.

Mother Teresa could be said to know the entire world. Appeals have come in to her from bishops all over asking her to set up foundations in their country. Paying heed to all of them, she personally supervises the installation of the Sisters, be it in the Americas, Australia, the Middle East, Asia, or Europe.

The jet is like a second cell to her. She prays there. Sometimes she talks about God to the person sitting next to her who is a complete stranger. She sinks herself in meditation. Tirelessly she undertakes each endless trip, hiking from trains to crowded buses, spending nights in third-class compartments.

Lacking the money to make an indispensable trip, she once offered her services as a stewardess. Since then the Indian Minister of Transportation has given her a card which allows her free access on the train. In 1973 Indira Gandhi made her the gift of a permanent pass for travel with the Indian airline. She takes off for the least appeal. She need only learn that one of her Sisters is having difficulties and she will fly to her aid. Occasionally people have been immune to her magnetism. She has even met with unfriendly receptions upon arriving with her Sisters. Once, coming to Ranchi, she found a barricade across the road and was greeted with cries of "Go back

where you came from, Mother Teresa." On this occasion she returned home.

It was on one of these trips that she met with an accident. On a mountain road on her way to Darjeeling to help with the rescue of part of the city that had, at the beginning of the monsoon, just been destroyed by an avalanche, her car hit a truck head-on. Thrown into the windshield, she received a gash on her scalp, which required nineteen stitches. She came dangerously close to losing an eye. Since she could no longer travel everywhere as often as she would have wished, she wrote. Bushels of letters. She knows every one of the Pro-

fessed Sisters of her Congregation but, much to her regret, not every one of the novices and postulants.

Traveling is one of her required tasks. Like a shepherd, Teresa watches maternally over her flock. For her, as for God, each of her lambs is the most irreplaceable of beings, just as the poor themselves.

SOMEONE FASCINATING
FOR THE YOUNG

Young persons and children, fascinated by Mother Teresa, respond to her with warmth and respect. Anyone who observes her together with the young today, will realize that she must have been a fine teacher, with an unusual empathy for

her pupils. Young women, and young men, from all walks of life and all parts of the world apply in great numbers for admission to the Missionaries of Charity. And wherever she goes, Teresa is likely to have a group of youngsters about her. She knows how to deal with the troublesome as well as the devoted. The story is told that, in her early years with the Missionaries, youthful vandals kept making trouble at one of the clinics. Finally Mother Teresa confronted them, alone, challenging them to kill her if that was what they wanted, but to leave the Missionaries unmolested in their work. The delinquents reportedly backed down at once and troubled her work no more.

Rigi-Scheidegg 20.4.1979

Liebe Mutter Theresia.
Es ist wundervoll, was du für die Menschen tust.
Wir finden es grossartig, dass du den Menschen dein (geopfert)
Leben opferst. Wir möchten Dir herzlich Danken
für deine Arbeit, und dass du den Menschen wieder
Hoffnung gibst.
Wir hoffen dass du noch lange Nächstenliebe aus-
üben kannst.

Wir grüssen Dich herzlich

Amadeo V.
Urs H.
Martin O.
Peter S.
Markus R.
Vreni Raunec

Urtilager   Rigi-Klösterli, 20.4.1979

Liebe Mutter Theresa!

Ist Dir Jesus schon einmal begegnet? Wir glauben, er ist
Dir schon begegnet oder er hat schon mit Dir gesprochen. Du
könntest doch sonst die grosse Kraft gar nicht finden.
   Wir freuen uns auch sehr, dass Du diesen armen und
elenden Menschen in Kalkutta hilfst. Wir hoffen, dass du
genug Geld für Essen und Betten sammeln kannst.
   Wir haben beschlossen, dass wir in unserer Gruppe "Kro-
kofant" Geld sammeln und wir schicken es Dir.

Wir hoffen Du kannst noch viel helfen.

Liebe Grüsse

Pia Pizzino
Monika C.
Martin Zünd
Denise Keller
Monika T
Myriam Colombo
A. Beer
Claudia Brander

She speaks to youth and children of all cultures, from the barefoot throngs in India (opposite page) to organized youth groups in the West such as the "Catholic Action" assembly that she is seen addressing in Rome (below). Thousands of children who have never seen her, work at collecting money for the Missionaries and send her letters and drawings. The affectionate portrait (opposite) by a West German child captures something essential in Teresa's radiance. The letters reproduced here are from two groups of Swiss schoolchildren. The one at left asks: "Did Jesus ever meet with you in person? We believe he has met you and spoken with you. Otherwise you could never have found this great strength." They go on to promise that they will collect funds for her in their town. In the flower-adorned letter above, children thank her for all that she has done. "We hope that you will continue for a long time to practice this love of your fellow man."

On leaving St. Mary's more than thirty years ago, Teresa turned her first attention to the children on the city streets. And children remain a fundamental element in the work of the Missionaries around the world, as well as in their fund-raising efforts.

Although many people do not give as much as they could, says Teresa:

"The new generation, especially the children, are understanding better. The children in England are making sacrifices to give a slice of bread to our children, and the

children of Denmark are making sacrifices to give a glass of milk to our children daily, and the children of Germany are making sacrifices to give one multi-vitamin daily to a child. These are the ways to greater love. These children when they grow up, they will have faith and love and a desire to serve and to give more."

In churches and schools all over the world, children are work-

ing and sacrificing to raise money for a form of charity that has captured their imagination more than any other. The Missionaries of Charity and Mother Teresa have stimulated schoolchildren to write letters and to make countless drawings. Shown here are a selection of drawings by thirteen and fourteen-year-old Danish children from the small isle of Als in the south of Denmark, who put together with younger children a book on life in India. They wrote two full-length

These nine drawings by eighth-grade children were made to illustrate a book they themselves wrote about the Missionaries of Charity. The story tells of two homeless children in Calcutta who are eventually saved by Teresa and the Missionaries. Along the way, many details of the Missionaries' work are captured in vivid, stirring images.
Upper row: *A nun shouts on discovering a live baby in a garbage can, as a rat leaps forth. One of the two heroes of the story is shown being welcomed at the orphanage.*
Lower row: *The Missionaries are seen feeding the sick who lie on the ground; tending a baby; with the dying; saving another baby in a garbage can; distributing food; bathing a child.*
Courtesy of Abbé Pierres Klunseres Forlag, Hellerup.

stories, which they illustrated themselves, about living conditions in India and about Mother Teresa's work in particular. The story from which these pictures are taken tells of two children in the slums of Calcutta who lead a difficult life until they finally find a home with the Missionaries. A teen-age girl in the story eventually joins the Missionaries as a nun.

This is just one example of a book about Teresa's work by and/or for children. The children of Als intend their book to be read by schoolchildren between the ages of ten and fifteen years. Although it is of course written in Danish, translations into other languages are planned.

AWARDS FOR TERESA AND HER WORK

The list of Mother Teresa's awards is impressive. She has won virtually all the great international prizes, and has had them presented to her by some of the most prominent persons in the world. But none of this has seemed to impress her unduly. Thanks to these awards, which almost always carry a large cash stipend, she can indulge her greatest joy in life: bringing a bit of happiness to the outcast and lonely. "Even the heads of state," she once remarked after receiving another of her prizes, "are God's children. A President, a pauper, a leper—they all need love and care."

Listed here are the prizes she is known to have won to date; some of the most famous ones are described in more detail in the following pages, with quotations from Mother Teresa's acceptance speeches.

1962	Padmachree ("Magnificent Lotus"), by the Indian Government
	Magsaysay Award for International Understanding, Philippines
1971	Pope John XXIII Peace Prize, by Pope Paul VI
	Good Samaritan Award, U.S.A
	John F. Kennedy International Award, U.S.A.
	Honorary Doctor of Humane Letters, Catholic University of America
1972	Jawaharlal Nehru Award for International Understanding, by the Indian Government
1973	Templeton Award for Progress in Religion, Great Britain
1974	"Mater et Magistra" Award, by the Third Order of St. Francis of Assisi, U.S.A.
	Honorary Doctorate, University of St. Francis Xavier, Canada
1975	FAO Ceres Medal, Rome
	Albert Schweitzer Prize, U.S.A.
	Twenty-fifth Anniversary Jubilee of the Missionaries of Charity celebrated in India, with honors from eighteen different religious denominations
1976	Honorary Doctorate, Santiniketan, India
1977	Honorary Doctor of Divinity, Cambridge University
1979	Balzan International Prize, Rome
	Honorary Doctorate, Temple University, U.S.A.
	Nobel Peace Prize, Oslo
1980	Bharat Ratna (Jewel of India), Indian Government

1962: PADMASHREE AWARD, INDIA

The first in a long string of honors and awards came to Teresa, fittingly, in her adopted homeland. "Padmashree" translates as Magnificent Lotus; it is a distinction awarded each year by the Indian government for outstanding services by a citizen. Though not the country's highest citation, the Padmashree was indeed an outstanding honor to be awarded to a simple nun, not even born in India, who lived in obscurity. The announcement of the award also caused no little stir.

The archbishop of Calcutta, startled at this unforeseen and rather irregular development, reportedly hesitated at first: should a nun be allowed to travel to Delhi, receive this award, and all the potentially head-swelling attention that would come with it? The whole thing seemed to smack too much of wordly vanity.

Finally it was decided that there was no danger of any such thing—not in Teresa's case. Her humility was felt, by all who knew her, to be more than equal to the challenge.

There remained only one problem: Mother Teresa herself wanted no part of the award. She was called to the archbishop to be advised in the matter. And thus it was that the policy was formed that was to guide her response to all the prizes and citations that were soon to come to her. This policy is that Teresa accepts awards not in her name, but in the name of all the sufferers of the world and all those who are trying to help.

"You must go, Mother," the archbishop reportedly told her, making her understand that the prize was something that would help the common effort. And so in September 1962, fourteen years after leaving St. Mary's, she made the journey to Delhi to be honored by the President of India for service to the poor. An important precedent had been set.

1962: MAGSAYSAY AWARD FOR INTERNATIONAL UNDERSTANDING, PHILIPPINES

No sooner had this nun broken with tradition by accepting the Padmashree from the Indian government, than she found herself cited for a second award. This prize set another precedent: with the Magsaysay Award for International Understanding, Teresa was being honored by a foreign government. She had become an international figure. And something of a world traveler. These precedents were going to become traditions for her.

This award was established by the Philippine government in memory of late President Ramón Magsaysay, a strong figure in the country's recent history, who governed from January 1954 until his death on 17 March 1957. President Magsaysay died when his plane crashed in the jungle near Asturias, on Cebu island. He had succeeded in bringing considerable stability and harmony to a country beset by guerrilla wars and party strife. The Philippines, which obtained its independence

Teresa's first official recognition outside India was the Magsaysay Prize awarded by the Philippine government in memory of the late President Ramón Magsaysay. The president was killed in an airplane crash in 1957, only three years after taking office. In the prize ceremony Teresa was cited as "the most meritorious woman of Asia" and awarded 50,000 rupees.

from the United States in 1946, had been ruled by Spain since the sixteenth century. The country is a republic and maintains strong western ties. Its population is 83 percent Catholic, quite unusual for an Asiatic country.

During her 1963 visit to receive the Magsaysay Award, Mother Teresa was received by the President and first lady of the Philippines. The authorities subsequently gave her every cooperation in the opening of two congregations of the Missionaries of Charity, in 1976 and 1977.

John XXIII, whose pontificate lasted from 1958 to 1963, a well-loved pope remembered for his humility, warmth, and awareness of the world's social realities.

1971: POPE JOHN XXIII PEACE PRIZE, ROME

Man has the right to live. He has the right to bodily integrity and to the means necessary for maintaining a decent standard of living.

POPE JOHN XXIII, *Pacem in Terris*, 1963

A singular honor for Teresa: Pope Paul VI hands her the first Pope John XXIII Peace Prize, in a ceremony in Rome on 6 January 1971, the Feast of the Epiphany, in recognition of her work among the poor and forgotten in India and the world.

After these first two awards, in late 1962, there were to be no others for more than eight years. These were of course years of intense activity, which saw Mother Teresa reaching out more and more beyond India, even while the Missionaries continued to expand operations inside the country as well. The Brothers were officially founded in 1963, the Missionaries became a society of pontifical right, under Pope Paul VI, on 1 February 1965, and congregations were opened in rapid succession in Caracas (1965), Ceylon (1967), Tanzania and Rome (1968), Australia (1969), Jordan (1970). The Co-Workers were set up and officially joined to the Missionaries in 1969, and the next year a noviciate was opened in London. By 1971 Mother Teresa had established a prospering order with branches on five continents, with hundreds of members and a sterling record of service to the needy. At this point she was selected for a prize that must have meant more than any other to her. In Rome, on 6 January 1971, Pope Paul VI conferred upon Teresa the Pope John XXIII Peace Prize, a newly created citation of which she was the first recipient. Whereas earlier awards had emanated from chiefs of state, this one was presented to her by His Holiness the Pope, head of the Church. And she received it in a special ceremony in Rome.

As she knelt down before Pope Paul on that Epiphany, His Holiness praised her for her work in the service of the poor, in the name of Christian love, and in the cause of peace. He presented Teresa a statue of the Madonna.

No small part of the enormous honor bestowed on her at this time was the evocation of the name John XXIII, whose example had inspired the creation of this peace prize. John, born in 1881, was pope for just five years (1958–1963) but left a decisive imprint on the Church. His pontificate is most remembered for two accomplishments: the historic Second Vatican Council (1962–1963), which brought about several reforms and a shift in emphasis, and his encyclical *Pacem in Terris* (Peace on Earth), which spoke out in favor of democracy, the right to resist social injustice, workers' rights, women's equality, rights of minorities, disarmament, and aid to underdeveloped countries. He was the pope who sought to promote understanding, to bridge gaps—between East and West, past and present, rich and poor, the church and the

world. And in this same spirit Mother Teresa can be said to merit the linking of her name and her work with those of Pope John XXIII.

* * *

In her speech accepting this prize, Mother Teresa evoked Pope John XXIII's call for peace on earth in his 1963 encyclical Pacem in Terris. *How, she asked, are we to go about attaining this peace?*

We must all work for Peace. Before we can win
this Peace, we must learn from Jesus to be gentle
and humble in our heart. Only humility will bring us
to Unity, and Unity to Peace. So let us help one
another to come so close to Christ that we will learn
the lesson of humility with joy.... Let us think
of the oppressed countries.
The greatest need in Bangladesh is for forgiveness.
There is so much bitterness and hate. You have no
idea how much these poor people have suffered.
If they feel that someone cares for them, that they are
loved, perhaps they will find it in their hearts
to forgive! I think this is the only thing that can
bring Peace.
We will all make this year especially a year of Peace.
To this end we will try to speak more to God and
with God, and less to men and with men. Let us
preach Christ's Peace as he has done. He did good
everywhere, he did not give up his good works just
because the Pharisees or others turned away from him,
and tried to ruin his Father's work. As Cardinal
Newman has written: Help me, wherever I go,
to spread Thy fragrance, let me preach it without
preaching, wordlessly, but by my example, by the
force of attraction, the very imitation of my acts,
the obvious fullness of the love that my heart feels
for Thee.

John Fitzgerald Kennedy (1917–1963), thirty-fifth president of the United States and the first Catholic to hold the office. A humanitarian award in his honor was created by his family and presented to Teresa for 1971.

1971: GOOD SAMARITAN AWARD, BOSTON

This year, 1971, was an important international year for Mother Teresa, not only where worldwide recognition of her work was concerned, but also in terms of the establishment of new centers abroad. It was indeed, in a sense, her "American year"—a year that saw the opening of the first American congregation of the Missionaries of Charity (The Bronx, New York, 19 October 1971), plus the awarding of two prizes in America and one honorary degree. The first of these prizes, the Good Samaritan Award, was presented to her in Boston in September 1971.

1971: JOHN F. KENNEDY INTERNATIONAL AWARD, USA

President Kennedy, who died in 1963, the same year as Pope John XXIII, was often associated with the late pope in the minds of Catholics. Both men had seemed to offer the promise of a more liberalizing tendency in their huge organizations—the Roman Catholic Church, and the American colossus. Now, having been praised for following in the footsteps of John XXIII in January 1971, Teresa was honored in the same year—16 October 1971—for exemplifying everything that was finest in the life and work of the late American president. One by one, all the great humanitarians both of this age and the past have been cited for comparison: Teresa is often likened to St. Francis, St. Teresa of Lisieux, Albert Schweitzer, Mahatma Gandhi, Simone Veil, as well as Kennedy, John XXIII, and others.

1971: DOCTOR OF HUMANE LETTERS, CATHOLIC UNIVERSITY, WASHINGTON

The first of her honorary university degrees—she has so far received a total of five—was awarded in the United States, at the Catholic University of America, Washington, D.C., on 28 October 1971.

1972: JAWAHARLAL NEHRU AWARD FOR INTERNATIONAL UNDERSTANDING, NEW DELHI

The Indian government created this annual award, in memory of late Prime Minister Jawaharlal Nehru, in 1966: "The Award shall be given for outstanding contribution to the promotion of international understanding, goodwill, and friendship among peoples of the world. Only recent work achieved within five years immediately preceding the nomination shall be considered for the Award." The prize brings the amount of 100,000 Indian rupees and a citation.

Teresa received this outstanding award from the president of India on 15 November 1972, although the prize was actually for the year 1969. The delay in the actual ceremony may have been due to her constant traveling in 1971!

Like all the distinctions that have been paid her, this Nehru Award has a specific character which sheds light on one particular aspect of Mother Teresa's achievement and the way it

Jawaharlal Nehru (1889–1964), the first prime minister of independent India, from 1947 until his death. He is remembered above all as a leader of the Nonaligned Nations Movement and as one of the architects of Indian autonomy.

is perceived internationally. She had been honored for service to India (Padmashree) and for Christian aid to her fellowman (Good Samaritan), as well as for contributing to the cause of peace (John XXIII Prize). This Nehru prize, like the Magsaysay Award, was given her specifically for having promoted international understanding.

If some of these awards were primarily religious in nature, the

The first Templeton Prize was presented to her by Prince Philip in a ceremony at London's Guildhall on 25 April 1973. The award includes a cash stipend of 34,000 pounds sterling. Teresa announced that the money would go toward the work with lepers undertaken by the Missionaries of Charity.

All those attending the ceremony, and especially the luncheon that followed, were struck by the contrast offered by Mother Teresa and Prince Philip whenever the tiny sunburned nun and the towering regal prince consort were side by side. Yet the two of them seem to have got along fine and engaged in a steady conversation. "Prince Philip was charming," Teresa later remarked to a friend. "He had kind words to say about our Institute. During the meal he inquired about our work and I told him what we do and why we do it."

Teresa also reported that the gala luncheon served in her honor was in fact a simple one, with only a single course. She believed that the organizers had wanted to show awareness for her work among the poor by avoiding ostentation.

In her acceptance speech, Mother Teresa stressed the need for human beings in all parts of the world to extend love to one another. It is a need, she said, that is felt not only in poorer countries:

Nehru prize has reference to world politics—more specifically to the transcendence of politics and of political strife. The late prime minister is remembered not only as a leader within India, but also—and perhaps especially—as an international figure who dealt on equal terms with the superpowers and the leaders of the major world blocs. Nehru, along with Marshal Tito of Yugoslavia and Egypt's President Nasser, created the International Nonaligned Movement, the association that made the Third World a political reality of some weight. The spirit of Nehru stands for the rights of former colonies, the so-called developing nations, who want no part in the disputes between East and West but stand for international order, law, respect, and peace. This spirit remains an integral part of India's political outlook—as it has of Yugoslavia's attitude. And Teresa, born in Yugoslavia and now an Indian citizen, has remained true to this spirit in everything she does.

1973: TEMPLETON PRIZE FOR PROGRESS IN RELIGION, LONDON

The Templeton Foundation, created by an American businessman to encourage religious devotion, decided in 1972 to fund an annual award to honor leaders in religion. They chose as first recipient Mother Teresa of Calcutta. Teresa was selected among two thousand nominees of various nationalities and religions, by an international jury of ten religious leaders. Because each juror represented a different religious group, the naming of Teresa for the award represented a truly ecumenical consensus.

Let us thank God that Mr. Templeton has had
the courage to give, for the glory of God, the capital
that Providence has so generously given him . . . .
In England and other places, in Calcutta,
in Melbourne, in New York, we find lonely people
who are known by the number of their room. Why
are we not there? Do we really know that there are
some people, maybe next-door to us? Maybe there
is a blind man who would be happy if you would
read the newspaper for him; maybe there is a rich
person who has no one to visit him—he has plenty
of other things, he is nearly drowned in them, but
there is not that touch and he needs your touch.
Some time back a very rich man came to our place,
and he said to me: "Please, either you or somebody,
come to my house. I am nearly half-blind and my wife

is nearly mental; our children have all gone abroad, and we are dying of loneliness, we are longing for the loving sound of a human voice." Let us not be satisfied with just giving money. Money is not enough, money can be got, but they need your hearts to love them. So, spread love everywhere you go: first of all in your own home. Give love to your children, to your wife or husband, to a next-door neighbor.

General of the Food and Agriculture Organization—a reminder that along with her work in such spheres as medical care, religion, and education, Mother Teresa and the Missionaries also play an important economic role in the world, feeding many thousands who would otherwise go hungry and thus effecting, at least to some extent, a redistribution of the world's wealth and its bounty.

1975: F. A. O. CERES MEDAL, ROME

The United Nations Food and Agricultural Organization, created in 1945, exists for the purpose of increasing world agricultural production and raising the standard of living throughout the world. In 1975 the organization chose to honor Mother Teresa "as a token of recognition for her exemplary commitment to the hungry and poor of the world." The F. A. O. created a new Ceres Medal (named after the goddess of fertility, associated with grain) depicting Mother Teresa on one side, her effigy surrounded by the words "Mother Teresa Ceres F. A. O. Rome" and a blade of wheat, while the other side, inscribed "Food for All, Holy Year 1975," showed a hungry child surrounded by two outstretched hands which have placed a bowl in front of him. This medal was presented to Mother Teresa in Rome in August 1975 by Edouard Saouma of Lebanon, Director-

1976: HONORARY DOCTORATE, INDIA

At the Indian national university (Santiniketan Visva-Bharati University), Mother Teresa received her third honorary doctoral degree, from the hand of Prime Minister Indira Gandhi, who has always been a fervent admirer of her work. Of all her many honors and awards, Teresa has received a total of four in India alone. One finds praise for her everywhere in her adopted country today, even if her road has not always been so easy (at one time she was accused, falsely, of trying to convert all the unfortunates who came her way). Typical was the comment made about her by the *Deccan Herald* in Bangalore:

"It is given to few human beings to create their own mythology, to establish here on earth their own pre-emptive right to immortality. Mother Teresa has become a saint and a legend in her own lifetime through a life dedicated to the service of the lowliest of the low."

1977: DOCTOR HONORIS CAUSA, CAMBRIDGE

An honory doctoral degree from Cambridge University, surely one of the world's most coveted distinctions, was added to Teresa's long string of international awards in a ceremony at the University on 10 June 1977. She received the

The doors of academe were thrown wide for Teresa yet again in 1977 when Cambridge University bestowed upon her an honorary Doctor of Divinity degree. This was her fourth honorary doctorate, after similar honors in the United States, Canada, and India. Her sari is covered here with the academic gown and scarf of the Doctor of Divinity, but the protruding foot seen below is still shod in her traditional sandal.

degree of honorary Doctor of Divinity from Prince Philip, who had also bestowed upon her the Templeton Prize four years before.

Prince Philip discussed, in his address on this occasion, the significance of honorary degrees:

It may be true that no useful purpose is served by presenting honorary degress, but how else can a university community demonstrate its corporate admiration and express its esteem for people it believes have made particularly valuable contributions to human civilization? After all, universities exist for the purpose of raising standards of human understanding and competence, so it seems only reasonable to wish to honor those who have achieved that purpose with conspicuous success.

Teresa's contribution was described by the University Orator, Dr. Frank Stubbings, in these terms:

She saw the multitudes and had compassion on them. With the permission of her superiors she went alone, in poverty—the five rupees she had with her could hardly be called wealth—to the homes of the poorest, tended their illnesses, set up a school in the midst of the slums.

1979: BALZAN INTERNATIONAL PRIZE, ROME

In a ceremony at the National Academy in Rome on 1 March 1979, Mother Teresa was awarded the 1978 Balzan Prize for humanitarianism, peace, and brotherhood among nations. The award, which carries a stipend of some $325,000, was given to Teresa for "the exceptional abnegation with which she has dedicated her whole life to aiding, in India and other countries of the world, the victims of hunger, misery, and illness, the abandoned and the dying, transforming into tireless action her love for suffering humanity."

The recipient of this award is chosen each year by the general prize committee of the E. Balzan International Foundation, based in Rome. This organization, established in 1962 according to a provision in the will of Angelena Balzan Danieli,

Cited for her tireless efforts on behalf of "Humanitarianism, peace, and brotherhood throughout the world," Teresa was honored in March 1979 with the 1978 Balzan Prize, presented by Italian President Sandro Pertini. Pope John Paul II also received her in a special audience during her brief stay in Rome, where she has won several of her awards. Seen in the rear, far right, is her brother Lazar.

promotes culture, science, and "the most meritorious initiatives of humanitarianism, peace, and brotherhood throughout the world." Mother Teresa, accepting the award, called it "a wonderful gift to the poor" and promised to use it in serving "the poorest of the poor." She was congratulated by Italian President Sandro Pertini, and was also received by Pope John Paul II in a special audience during her visit in Rome to accept this award. Exciting as it was, however, this international prize was soon to be eclipsed by one far greater before the year's end.

1979: HONORARY DOCTORATE, TEMPLE UNIVERSITY, PHILADELPHIA

On 16 July 1979, Mother Teresa received yet another honorary doctorate, her fifth—and the second to be awarded in the United States. She is shown receiving this degree, at Temple University, Philadelphia, beside Cardinal Krol (at left). Her visits to the United States since 1971 have been frequent. They included attendance at the Eucharistic Conference, also in Philadelphia, in 1976, and a special reception in her honor by the association of Americans of Albanian descent. "My prayer," she told this group in Philadelphia, "is that you and I and all the people of Albania the whole world over become holy.... Holiness is a very simple duty for you and me."

THE NOBEL PEACE PRIZE: FROM HENRI DUNANT TO MOTHER TERESA

Four of the Nobel Peace Prize recipients offer close parallels with the humanitarian work done by Teresa and the Missionaries of Charity: the founder of the Red Cross, Henri Dunant; a man who aided refugees, Fridtjof Nansen; the medical doctor Albert Schweitzer; and the champion of civil rights, Martin Luther King, Jr.

Fridtjof Nansen

Albert Schweitzer

Martin Luther King, Jr.

1901 Jean Henri Dunant
Frédéric Passy

1902 Elie Ducommun
Charles Albert Gobat

1903 Sir William Cremer

1904 Institute of International
Law

1905 Baroness von Suttner

1906 Theodore Roosevelt

1907 Ernesto Teodoro Moneta
Louis Renault

1908 Klas Pontus Arnoldson
Frederik Bajer

1909 Baron d'Estournelles
de Constant
Auguste Beernaert

1910 International Peace Bureau

1911 Tobias Asser
Alfred Fried

1912 Elihu Root

1913 Henri Lafontaine

1917 International Red Cross
Committee

1919 Woodrow Wilson

1920 Léon Bourgeois

1921 Karl Branting
Christian Louis Lange

1922 Fridtjof Nansen

1925 Sir Austen Chamberlain
Charles Gates Dawes

1926 Aristide Briand
Gustav Stresemann

1927 Ferdinand Buisson
Ludwig Quidde

1929 Frank B. Kellogg

1930 Nathan Söderblom

1931 Jane Addams
Nicholas Murray Butler

1933 Sir Norman Angell

1934 Arthur Henderson

1935 Carl von Ossietzky

1936 Carlos Saavedra Lamas

1937 Viscount Cecil of Chelwood

1938 Nansen International Office
for Refugees

1944 International Red Cross
Committee

1945 Cordell Hull

1946 Emily Greene Balch
John R. Mott

1947 American Friends' Service
Committee
Friends' Service Council

1949 Lord Boyd-Orr

1950 Ralph Bunche

1951 Léon Jouhaux

1952 Albert Schweitzer

1953 Georges Catlett Marshall

1954 Office of the UN High
Commissioner for Refugees
(UNHCR)

1957 Lester Bowles Pearson

1958 Georges Pire

1959 Philip Noel-Baker

1960 Albert John Lutuli

1961 Dag Hammerskjöld

1962 Linus Carl Pauling

1963 International Red Cross
Committee

1964 Martin Luther King, Jr.

1965 UN Children's Fund
(UNICEF)

1968 René Cassin

1969 International Labour
Organisation (ILO)

1970 Norman Ernest Borlaug

1971 Willy Brandt

1973 Henry Kissinger
Le Duc Tho

1974 Eisaku Sato
Sean MacBride

1975 Andrej Sacharov

1976 Betty Williams
Mairead Corrigan

1977 Amnesty International

1978 Anwar el Sadat
Menachem Begin

1979 Mother Teresa

THE GREAT EVENT: OSLO 1979

Mother Teresa arrives in Oslo, in December 1979, for the official Nobel Prize ceremonies. Even before she set foot on Norwegian soil, the drama had begun: the contrast between this humble nun in her simple dress, carrying her own sparse belongings, and the glittering world of international pomp and circumstance. Throughout the Nobel rites, all the receptions and the speeches, Teresa remained simple and unaffected.

"Personally I am unworthy. I accept in the name of the poor, because I believe that by giving me the prize they've recognized the presence of the poor in the world." So said Mother Teresa in October 1979 on first learning of the Nobel Committee's decision.

If she felt unworthy, it was difficult, in the aftermath of the Committee's announcement, to find anyone who agreed with that judgment. Journalists, authors, and public figures had been urging a Nobel Peace Prize for Mother Teresa for years. Senator Edward Kennedy officially proposed her for the honor in 1975, shortly after the award to U.S. Secretary of State Henry Kissinger and North Vietnam representative Le Duc Tho in 1973 had caused such bitter press comment.

How much greater was the unanimous relief and delight six years later when Mother Teresa was finally given this honor. It would have been difficult to hear a dissenting voice. The general feeling was summed up in this editorial from *The Washington Post* (20 October 1979):

"Most of the recipients of the Nobel Peace Prize over the years have been politicians and diplomats. But Mother Teresa, the nun who founded the Missionaries of Charity, has spent the last 31 years working with the destitute and dying in the slums of Calcutta. It is the example of personal devotion to these people, as individuals, that is compelling. The award is, among other things, a reminder of a kind of poverty that most Europeans and Americans are unlikely ever to see. Occasionally, the Norwegian Nobel Committee uses the prize to remind the world that there is more than one kind of peace, and that politics is not the only way to pursue it."

The Statesman of New Delhi went even farther: "Seldom can an honor have been better deserved, or be more likely to be widely appreciated, than the award of the Nobel Peace Prize to Mother Teresa of Calcutta." For *The Times of India*, "It is comforting to know that the world still recognises virtue, that hope and compassion can dispel misery and cynicism, and that all the cherished values are as intact now as ever

Residents of Oslo still remembered the tension that had surrounded the Nobel ceremonies the previous year, when Israeli Premier Menachem Begin's arrival to receive his prize required stringent security measures. The ceremony had to be moved from the usual site to a medieval fortress. If, in 1979, President Carter, or a Soviet dissident, or the late South African black leader Steve Biko had won, security might once again have been a problem. But Teresa needed no bomb searches, helicopter surveillance, or armed guards. The uncontroversial ceremonies this year went on in a relaxed atmosphere marked by tangible admiration for the winner and all she represents. Teresa is seen in conversation with an official (left) and entering the hall of Oslo University (below), traditional site of the awards ceremony.

before unassailable by catastrophic folly. To her more than to any other person alive today mankind is beholden for the restoration of faith in itself."

For many persons throughout the world, the Nobel Prize Committee by selecting Teresa had passed a kind of test, proving its seriousness of purpose. It was as if the Nobel Com-

mittee had been more honored by Teresa than Teresa by the Committee. One Calcutta paper remarked, "The Nobel Prize Award Committee has proved its ability to rise above controversies, usually associated with its Peace Prize award, by choosing Mother Teresa for this year's Nobel Prize award."

105

All India seemed to rejoice when the word came, two months before the actual ceremony in Oslo, that Mother Teresa was to receive the Nobel Peace Prize. Before leaving for Oslo, she was honored in a special reception on 9 November 1979 by the Indian government. Indian Prime Minister Shri Charan Singh expressed his country's admiration for Teresa in these terms:

"Mother Teresa came to India fifty years ago. She wanted to serve the people of this country. Her choice turned out to be fortunate for the country.

"Many great persons have trod this earth. But very few good ones have—and Mother Teresa is one of them.

"In India alone she looks after 56,000 lepers, besides a large number of the poor and the unwanted. It will take either a Shakespeare or a Milton to record her services to India. Indeed, her services to humanity as a whole are beyond compare."

The External Affairs Minister, Shri Shyam Nandan Mishra, added his own encomium:

"The work done by her order of sisters, the Missionaries of Charity, now encompasses not only India but four continents. The hope and succour she has brought to the suffering, the destitute, the poor and the forlorn is but a reflection of her idealism which has triumphed over materialistic insularity; of a service that seeks no rewards; of a mission that finds fulfilment in wiping out the tears from every eye as Mahatma Gandhi sought to do.

"To such a one honours and recognitions come as leaves and blossoms come to trees and are but humanity's tribute to the Supreme. The Nobel Peace Prize now awarded to her, follows the Nehru Award and climaxes the numerous honours that have come to her from the Church and from the world of academia. All these awards and honours are merely the affirmation of love as the highest truth, and service as the highest pleasure."

In a spontaneous outburst of esteem and affection, the people of Oslo turned out in sub-freezing temperatures to greet Teresa on her arrival in their city.

Professor John Sanness, chairman of the Norwegian Nobel Committee, made the official address announcing the award of the Peace Prize to Mother Teresa and presented the prize to her (below). The prize includes a purse of $ 190,000, which Teresa announced would be used by the lepers and destitute to whom she has dedicated her life. "Thank God," she said, "for this gift for the poor. God's blessing will be with the people who have given the prize. I hope it will be a real means of bringing peace and happiness in the world of today."

by Fridtjof Nansen: "Love of one's neighbor is realistic policy."
As a description of Mother Teresa's life's work we might select the slogan that a previous Nobel Peace Prize laureate, Albert Schweitzer, adopted as the leitmotif for his own work: "Veneration for life"....
The Norwegian Nobel Committee is delighted to note this impressive and steadily growing scope of the work undertaken by the Order.

From the speech delivered by Professor John Sanness, Chairman of the Norwegian Nobel Committee, on the occasion of the award of the Nobel Peace Prize for 1979, Oslo, December 10, 1979:

Your Majesty, Your Royal Highnesses, Your Excellencies, Ladies and Gentlemen:
The Norwegian Nobel Committee has awarded the Peace Prize for 1979 to Mother Teresa....
The Norwegian Nobel Committee has considered it right and appropriate, precisely in this year, in their choice of Mother Teresa, to remind the world of the words spoken

With her message she is able to reach through to something innate in every human mind—if for no other purpose than to create a potential, a seed for good. If this were not the case, the world would be deprived of hope, and work for peace would have little meaning. It would, furthermore, be incompatible with Mother Teresa's own view of human beings, the men and women she serves because she wishes to serve Christ and approach more closely to Him....

THE NOBEL PRIZE ADDRESS

Having received the world's greatest honor, the tiny nun mounted the rostrum and delivered the address reprinted below in its entirety.

As we have gathered here together to thank God for the Nobel Peace Prize I think it will be beautiful that we pray the prayer of St. Francis of Assisi which always surprises me very much—we pray this prayer every day after Holy Communion, because it is very fitting for each one of us, and I always wonder that so many hundreds of years ago as St. Francis of Assisi composed this prayer that they had the same difficulties that we have today, as we recite this prayer that fits very nicely for us also. I think some of you already have got it—so we will pray together. . . .

Let us thank God for the opportunity that we all have together today, for this gift of peace that reminds us that we have been created to live that peace, and Jesus became man to bring that good news to the poor. He being God became man in all things like us except sin, and he proclaimed very clearly that he had come to give the good news. The news was peace to all of good will and this is something that we all want—the peace of heart—and God loved the world so much that he gave his son—it was a giving—it is as much as if to say it hurt God to give, because he loved the world so much that he gave his son, and he gave him to Virgin Mary, and what did she do with him?

As soon as he came in her life—immediately she went in haste to give that good news, and as she came into the house of her cousin, the child—the unborn child—the child in the womb of Elizabeth, lit with joy. He, that little unborn child, was the first messenger of peace. He recognized the Prince of Peace, he recognized that Christ has come to bring the good news for you and for me. And as if that was not enough—it was not enough to become a man—he died on the cross to show that greater love, and he died for you and for me and for that leper and for that man dying of hunger and that naked person lying in the street not only of Calcutta, but of Africa, and New York, and London, and Oslo—and insisted that we love one another as he loves each one of us. And we read that in the Gospel very clearly—love as I have loved you—as I love you—as the Father has loved me, I love you—and the harder the Father loved him, he gave him to us, and how much we love one another, we, too, must give to each other until it hurts. It is not enough for us to say: I love

God, but I do not love my neighbor. St. John says you are a liar if you say you love God and you don't love your neighbor. How can you love God whom you do not see, if you do not love your neighbor whom you see, whom you touch, with whom you live. And so this is very important for us to realize that love, to be true, has to hurt. It hurt Jesus to love us, it hurt him. And to make sure we remember his great love he made himself bread of life to satisfy our hunger for his love. Our hunger for God, because we have been created for that love. We have been created in his image. We have been created to love and be loved, and then he has become man to make it possible for us to love as he loved us. He makes himself the hungry one—the naked one—the homeless one—the sick one—the one in prison—the lonely one—the unwanted one—and he says: You did it to me. Hungry for our love, and this is the hunger of our poor people. This is the hunger that you and I must find, it may be in our own home.

I never forget an opportunity I had in visiting a home where they had all these old parents of sons and daughters who had just put them in an institution and forgotten maybe. And I went there, and I saw in that home they had everything, beautiful things, but everybody was looking towards the door. And I did not see a single one with their smile on their face. And I turned to the sister and I asked: How is that? How is it that the people they have everything here, why are they all looking towards the door, why are they not smiling? I am so

used to see the smile on our people, even the dying ones smile, and she said: This is nearly every day, they are expecting, they are hoping that a son or daughter will come to visit them. They are hurt because they are forgotten, and see—this is where love comes. That poverty comes right there in our own home, even neglect to love. Maybe in our own family we have somebody who is feeling lonely, who is feeling sick, who is feeling worried, and these are difficult days for everybody. Are we there, are we there to receive them, is the mother there to receive the child?

I was surprised in the waste to see so many young boys and girls given into drugs, and I tried to find out why—why is it like that, and the answer was: Because there is no one in the family to receive them. Father and mother are so busy they have no time. Young parents are in some institution and the child takes back to the street and gets involved in something. We are talking of peace. These are things that break peace, but I feel the greatest destroyer of peace today is abortion, because it is a direct war, a direct killing—direct murder by the mother herself. And we read in the Scripture, for God says very clearly: Even if a mother could forget her child—I will not forget you—I have curved you in the palm of my hand. We are curved in the palm of His hand, so close to Him that unborn child has been curved in the hand of God. And that is what strikes me most, the beginning of that sentence, that even if a mother could forget, something impossible—but even if she could forget—I will not forget you. And today the greatest means—the greatest destroyer of Peace is abortion. And we who are standing here—our parents wanted us. We would not be here if our parents would do that to us. Our children, we want them, we love them, but what of the millions? Many people are very, very concerned with the children in India, with the children of Africa where quite a number die, maybe of malnutrition, of hunger and so on, but millions are dying deliberately by the will of the mother. And this is what is the greatest destroyer of peace today. Because if a mother can kill her own child—what is left for me to kill you and you to kill me—there is nothing between. And this I appeal in India, I appeal everywhere: Let us bring the child back, and this year being the child's year: What have we done for the child?

At the beginning of the year I told, I spoke everywhere and I said: Let us make this year that we make every single child born, and unborn, wanted. And today is the end of the year, have we really made the children wanted? I will give you something terrifying. We are fighting abortion by adoption, we have saved thousands of lives, we have sent words to all the clinics, to the hospitals, police stations—please don't destroy the child, we will take the child. So every hour of the day and night it is always somebody, we have quite a number of unwedded mothers—tell them come, we will take care of you, we will take the child from you, and we will get a home for the child. And we have a tremendous demand for families who have no children, that is the blessing of God for us. And also, we are doing another thing which is very beautiful— we are teaching our beggars, our leprosy patients, our slum dwellers, our people of the street, natural family planning. And in Calcutta alone in six years—it is all in Calcutta—we have had 61,273 babies less from the families who would have had, but because they practise this natural way of abstaining, of self-control, out of love for each other. We teach them the temperature meter which is very beautiful, very simple, and our poor people understand. And you know what they have told me? Our family is healthy, our family is united, and we can have a baby whenever we want. So clear—those people in the street, those beggars—and I think that if our people can do like that how much more you and all the others who can know the ways and means without destroying the life that God has created in us. The poor people are very great people. They can teach us so many beautiful things. The other day one of them came to thank us and said: You people who have evolved chastity you are the best people to teach us family planning. Because it is nothing more than self-control out of love for each other. And I think they said a beautiful sentence. And these are people who maybe have nothing to eat, maybe they have not a home where to live, but they are great people. The poor are very wonderful people. One evening we went out and we picked up four people from the street. And one of them was in a most terrible condition—and I told the sisters: You take care of the other three, I take this one that looked worse. So I did for her all that my love can do. I put her in bed, and

there was such a beautiful smile on her face. She took hold of my hand, said one word: Thank you—and died. I could not help but examine my conscience before her, and I asked what would I say if I was in her place. And my answer was very simple. I would have tried to draw a little attention to myself, I would have said I am hungry, that I am dying, I am cold, I am in pain, or something, but she gave me much more—she gave me her grateful love. And she died with a smile on her face. As that man said whom we picked up from the drain, half eaten with worms, and we brought him to the home: I have lived like an animal in the street, but I am going to die like an angel, loved and cared for. And it was so wonderful to see the greatness of that man who could speak like that, who could die like that without blaming anybody, without cursing anybody, without comparing anything. Like an angel— this is the greatness of our people. And that is why we believe what Jesus has said: I was hungry—I was naked—I was homeless—I was unwanted, unloved, uncared for—and you did it to me. I believe that we are not real social workers. We may be doing social work in the eyes of the people, but we are really contemplatives in the heart of the world. For we are touching the body of Christ 24 hours. We have 24 hours in this presence, and so you and I. You too try to bring that presence of God in your family, for the family that prays together stays together. And I think that we in our family, we don't need bombs and guns, to destroy to bring peace—just get together, love one another, bring that peace, that joy, that strength of presence of each other in the home. And we will be able to overcome all the evil that is in the world. There is so much suffering, so much hatred, so much misery, and we with our prayer, with our sacrifice are beginning at home. Love begins at home, and it is not how much we do, but how much love we put in the action that we do. It is to God Almighty—how much we do it does not matter, because He is infinite, but how much love we put in that action. How much we do to Him in the person that we are serving. Some time ago in Calcutta we had great difficulty in getting sugar, and

112

*I don't know how the word got around to the children, and
a little boy of four years old, Hindu boy, went home and
told his parents: I will not eat sugar for three days, I will give
my sugar to Mother Teresa for her children. After three
days his father and mother brought him to our house. I had
never met them before, and this little one could scarcely
pronounce my name, but he knew exactly what he had come
to do. He knew that he wanted to share his love. And this
is why I have received such a lot of love from you all. From
the time that I have come here I have simply been surrounded
with love, and with real, real understanding love. It could
feel as if everyone in India, everyone in Africa is somebody
very special to you. And I felt quite at home I was telling Sister
today. I feel in the Convent with the Sisters as if I am in
Calcutta with my own Sisters. So completely at home here,
right here. And so here I am talking with you—I want you
to find the poor here, right in your own home first. And begin
love there. Be that good news to your own people. And find out
about your nextdoor neighbor—do you know who they are?
I had the most extraordinary experience with a Hindu family
who had eight children. A gentleman came to our house and
said: Mother Teresa, there is a family with eight children, they
had not eaten for so long—do something. So I took some rice
and I went there immediately. And I saw the children—their
eyes shining with hunger—I don't know if you have ever seen
hunger. But I have seen it very often. And she took the rice, she
divided the rice, and she went out. When she came back
I asked her—where did you go, what did you do? And she
gave me a very simple answer: They are hungry also. What
struck me most was that she knew—and who are they,
a Muslim family— and she knew. I didn't bring more rice that
evening because I wanted them to enjoy the joy of sharing.
But there were those children, radiating joy, sharing the joy
with their mother because she had the love to give. And you see
this is where love begins—at home, and I want you—and
I am very grateful for what I have received. It has been
a tremendous experience and I go back to India—I will be back
by next week, the 15th I hope—and I will be able to bring
your love.
And I knew well that you have not given from your abundance,
but you have given until it has hurt you. Today the little
children they gave—I was so surprised—there is so much joy
for the children that are hungry. That the children like
themselves will need love and care and tenderness, like they
get so much from their parents. So let us thank God that
we have had this opportunity to come to know each other, and
this knowledge of each other has brought us very close. And we
will be able to help not only the children of India and Africa,
but will be able to help the children of the whole world,
because as you know our Sisters are all over the world.
And with this Prize that I have received as a Prize of Peace,
I am going to try to make the home for many people that have
no home. Because I believe that love begins at home, and if we
can create a home for the poor—I think that more and more love
will spread. And we will be able through this understanding
love to bring peace, be the good news to the poor. The poor
in our own family first, in our country and in the world.
To be able to do this, our Sisters, our lives have to be woven
with prayer. They have to be woven with Christ to be able to
understand, to be able to share. Because today there is so much
suffering—and I feel that the passion of Christ is being
relived all over again—are we there to share that passion,
to share that suffering of people. Around the world, not only
in the poor countries, but I found the poverty of the West
so much more difficult to remove. When I pick up a person
from the street, hungry, I give him a plate of rice, a piece
of bread, I have satisfied. I have removed that hunger. But a
person that is shut out, that feels unwanted, unloved, terrified,
the person that has been thrown out from society—that poverty
is so hurtable and so much, and I find that very difficult.
Our Sisters are working amongst that kind of people in the
West. So you must pray for us that we may be able to be that
good news, but we cannot do that without you, you have to do
that here in your country. You must come to know the poor,
maybe our people here have material things, everything, but
I think that if we all look into our own homes, how difficult
we find it sometimes to smile at each other, and that the smile
is the beginning of love. And so let us always meet each other
with a smile, for the smile is the beginning of love, and once
we begin to love each other naturally we want to do something.*

So you pray for our Sisters and for me and for our Brothers, and for our co-workers that are around the world. That we may remain faithful to the gift of God, to love Him and serve Him in the poor together with you. What we have done we would not have been able to do if you did not share with your prayers, with your gifts, this continual giving. But I don't want you to give me from your abundance, I want that you give me until it hurts. The other day I received 15 dollars from a man who has been on his back for twenty years, and the only part that he can move is his right hand. And the only companion that he enjoys is smoking. And he said to me: I do not smoke for one week, and I send you this money. It must have been a terrible sacrifice for him, but see how beautiful, how he shared, and with that money I bought bread and I gave to those who are hungry with a joy on both sides, he was giving and the poor were receiving. This is something that you and I—it is a gift of God to us to be able to share our love with others. And let it be as it was for Jesus. Let us love one another as he loved us. Let us love Him with undivided love. And the joy of loving Him and each other—let us give now—that Christmas is coming so close. Let us keep that joy of loving Jesus in our hearts. And share that joy with all that we come in touch with. And that radiating joy is real, for we have no reason not to be happy because we have Christ with us. Christ in our hearts, Christ in the poor that we meet, Christ in the smile that we give and the smile that we receive. Let us make that one point: That no child will be unwanted, and also that we meet each other always with a smile, especially when it is difficult to smile.

I never forget some time ago about 14 professors came from the United States from different universities. And they came to Calcutta to our house. Then we were talking about that they had been to the home for the dying. We have a home for the dying in Calcutta, where we have picked up more than 36,000 people only from the streets of Calcutta, and out of that big number more than 18,000 have died a beautiful death. They have just gone home to God; and they came to our house and we talked of love, of compassion, and then one of them asked me: Say, Mother, please tell us something that we will remember, and I said to them: Smile at each other, make time for each other in your family. Smile at each other. And then another one asked me: Are you married, and I said: Yes, and I find it sometimes very difficult to smile at Jesus because he can be very demanding sometimes. This is really something true, and there is where love comes—when it is demanding, and yet we can give it to Him with joy. Just as I have said today, I have said that if I don't go to Heaven for anything else I will be going to Heaven for all the publicity because it has purified me and sacrificed me and made me really something ready to go to Heaven. I think that this is

something, that we must live life beautifully, we have Jesus with us and He loves us. If we could only remember that God loves me, and I have an opportunity to love others as he loves me, not in big things, but in small things with great love, then Norway becomes a nest of love. And how beautiful it will be that from here a centre for peace has been given. That from here the joy of life of the unborn child comes out. If you become a burning light in the world of peace, then really the Nobel Peace Prize is a gift of the Norwegian people. God bless you!

1980: THE JEWEL OF INDIA, NEW DELHI

No sooner had Mother Teresa received her Nobel Prize and returned home, than another prize was announced. The Indian government had decided to award her its highest honor, Bharat Ratna (the Jewel of India). This was, then, the fourth of her national awards in India, following the Padmachree in 1962, the Nehru Award in 1972, the honorary doctorate in 1976, not to mention a celebration in honor of the Missionaries' twenty-fifth anniversary (1975) and the reception to celebrate the Nobel Prize announcement.

Thus, in a simple civil investiture ceremony at Ashoka Hall of Rashtrapati Bhavan (the presidential palace), on 22 March 1980, the president of India, N. Sanjiva Reddy, conferred the Bharat Ratna upon the "Saint of the Gutters." Mother Teresa said she was receiving the award on behalf of all men and women who had dedicated themselves to the service of the poor and suffering all over the country, and stressed that she accepted this prize "in the name of all religions."

India's decision to confer its highest civilian honor on Mother Teresa reflected not only the country's appreciation of her efforts, but also the great pride that Indians take in her. As is shown in the words quoted at right from India's foreign minister Shri Shyam Nandan Mishra, Mother Teresa is that rare phenomenon: a prophet *with* honor in her own country.

"She embodies in herself compassion and love of humanity as few in history have done: Her presence in our midst gives to the capital city of India a touch of divine grace and utter humility which is symbolic of our tradition. Her entire life has been a personification of service and compassion. These are the imperatives of human existence which are generally affirmed in words but denied in action."

Back in India, a new honor awaited her. President N. Sanjiva Reddy presented her, in March 1980, the country's highest civilian honor, the Bharat Ratna (Jewel of India). This award follows a whole series of outstanding honors bestowed on Teresa by her adopted country.

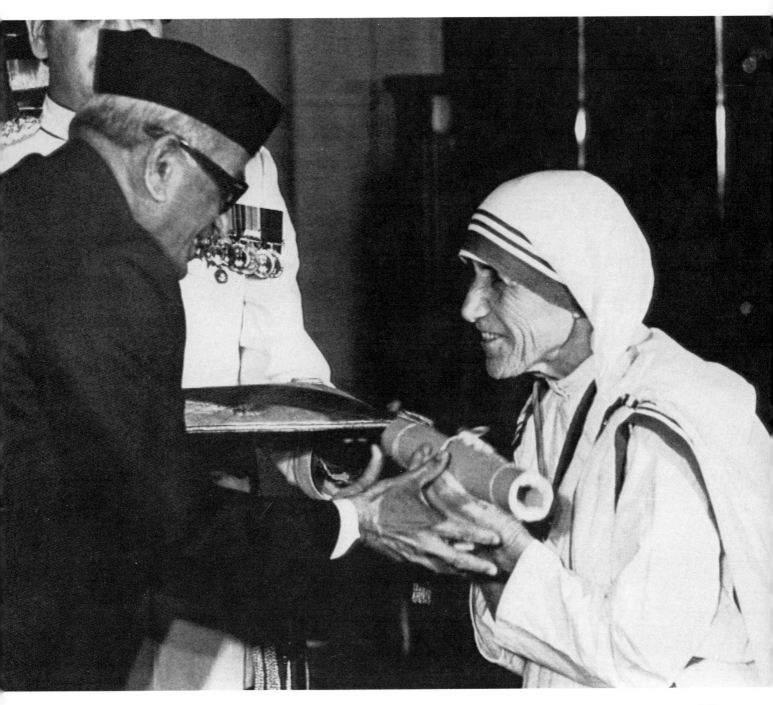

HOMAGE TO MOTHER TERESA

Two champions of the poor: Teresa is shown with Archbishop Helder Pessoa Camâra of Recife (in northeastern Brazil), who has for years been calling for the birth of a "Church of the poor." The controversial prelate has led a "liberation" movement in the Latin American Church, with an emphasis on grassroots action among the lowest social levels. This movement has organized literacy classes for the poor and "consciousness-raising groups" to build morale and solidarity among the people that, many believe, the official Church had failed. Archbishop Helder Camâra, though far more controversial politically, has a great deal in common with Mother Teresa. Both have sought, by their personal commitment, to go directly to the neediest and most neglected, translating the Gospel message into concrete action. When contacted by the author of this book, Helder Camâra very graciously contributed the comment on Mother Teresa printed at left.

If young persons reach the conclusion that the Church prides itself on writing beautiful speeches and remarkable resolutions, but lacks the courage to bring these words to life, then our youth will turn their back on the Church and embark on the worst kinds of radicalism. Fortunately the Spirit of God watches over Christ's Church, despite the weakness of the men and women of the Church. The Spirit of God, yes, embodied in individuals such as Mother Teresa of Calcutta.
It is enough to have met her just once. She is unforgettable. It is not what she says that matters: the world is filled, and more than filled, with lovely words. What matters is what she is.

ARCHBISHOP HELDER CAMÂRA

She lives the truth that prayer is devotion, prayer is service. Service is her concern, her religion, her redemption. To meet her is to feel utterly humble, to sense the power of tenderness, the strength of love.

INDIRA GANDHI

Your longstanding noble activity and self-sacrificing fight against disease and poverty have, by this Nobel Prize, received their deserved affirmation which will, I believe, stimulate a greater interest for the well-being of man in the world.

PRESIDENT JOSEF TITO OF YUGOSLAVIA

Your work on behalf of children, refugees, the poor and the sick has been a great inspiration for many years to those of us who cherish and espouse human rights. Mankind is in your debt for your fine contributions and for the example you have provided of selfless concern for others.

PRESIDENT JIMMY CARTER OF THE UNITED STATES OF AMERICA

The news about the award of this honorable prize to you—to one who devotes her life to the service of the poor, the suffering, and the dying, has been appreciated unanimously in Germany. It is an encouragement to all these who follow your example.

PRESIDENT KARL CARSTENS OF THE FEDERAL REPUBLIC OF GERMANY

"AND NOW GET TO WORK"

Teresa's work goes on as before, says her brother, who still sees in the Nobel Prize laureate the pious, hardworking, witty girl of long ago. She may be a world-famous figure, but back at the Missionaries of Charity mother house in Calcutta, what counts is deeds rather than words, the poor and suffering rather than any one individual.

What effect, then, have all these honors and prizes had? They have one advantage: the world has become aware, through them, of Mother Teresa, and has seen what a lone individual, small though she be, is capable of. She has accepted all these prizes, in her inimitable way, in the name of the poor, declaring "I am not important."

What remains important is the suffering of humanity, the hungry, the ill, the lonely and dying. And she continues to render service and to spread her work across the world, from the headquarters in the mother house in Calcutta and the door marked "Mother M. Teresa" (pictured at right).

She shuns publicity today even more than before. Are there any other changes in Mother Teresa since the awarding of the Nobel Prize? We have asked the person who has known her longest, her brother Lazar Bojaxhiu (who shared his childhood memories on pages 24–26), to bring us up to date on Mother Teresa today.

"Mother Teresa and I meet regularly now—every year or two. This past year we got together more than once. We were in Rome to meet His Holiness last May, and my daughter and I were at her side in December in Oslo when she received the Nobel Prize. And we exchange letters.

"But for a long time we didn't meet. We couldn't. I finally saw her in the early nineteen-fifties, when her order was officially established by Pius XII.

"When we meet now, she always reminds me of our mother, though our mother was much taller. Our sister Aga looked more like our father. Teresa hasn't really changed. One thing: she has almost completely forgotten how to speak Albanian—though she still *writes* to me in Albanian. I imagine it takes her time to do that! But if she speaks it very little, she still remembers the old songs in Albanian, and we two sing together every time we meet.

"Today I call her 'Mother,' just as everybody else does. She *is* Mother Teresa now. But when I see her in action, I realize she is still the same sharp little girl, still part of the same family, and I recognize our parents' character and commitment, their idealism and discipline. She has built a worldwide organization from nothing. By her efforts alone—and the help she could persuade people to give her.

"When we were saying good-bye in Rome, I witnessed a typical incident. We were at the airport, she was leaving for Delhi. She and the other nuns with her had just been told that they couldn't carry their rough bundless with them—bundles of food, clothing, and God-knows-what that they had collected to take back to India, all wrapped up in newspapers, ragged cardboard, and strings. Piles and piles of the stuff. As I went to say good-bye to her, she and the other sisters were kneeling down in the middle of the airport—causing quite a scene, as you can imagine, with Italian customs officers everywhere waving their arms and arguing frantically with her. I asked her what was wrong. 'Oh, we're just kneeling down,' she said, 'to ask God to change the officials' mind so that we can carry these gifts to their destination.' I could hardly keep from laughing. And within three minutes two or three more uniformed officials appeared to say it would be all right after all, and to try to hurry the sisters along and get the scene over with. *That's* how she works.

"She always loved a joke, and she still does. In Rome, when she met up with some of her nuns, they were very upset, reporting that they had been robbed of some forty thousand lire. Just as she never worries about the future, always using the word 'Providence'—God will provide—so too she refused to cry about a loss or robbery. 'Don't give it another thought,' she told the nuns. 'It's only money. The only thing we have to worry about losing is *you*. And nobody's going to steal you, you know—you're much too ugly. Now come along and get to work.'"

THE GREATEST HONOR OF ALL

No one could have asked for more publicity, more fame, or more prizes and honors than Mother Teresa has received. And few could have turned their back on such glory and excitement, shrugged it off, and gone quietly back to work the way she has done since the height of the Nobel Prize fever. She has refused to grant further interviews and shunned all attempts to keep her name in the headlines.

It is impossible to say which of her many awards and citations may have touched her the most personally. Although all of them have been received in the name of the poor and of her co-workers, never for herself alone, surely there has been some degree of pleasure attached to each.

It is worth mentioning one more distinction that has been conferred on Teresa, one that no headlines have proclaimed and no television cameras have photographed. It was not bestowed on her by a Pope or a university or an international committee, but instead by anonymous residents of Calcutta. Not very far from the mother house of the Missionaries of Charity, people have erected a simple shrine on a patch of dirt beside the road. Amid the dust and noise and refuse, a small impromptu altar leans on a solitary tree-trunk. Flowers and candles are offered here, in front of statuettes of Mary and Jesus. And, hanging on the tree by the altar, the pious street people of Calcutta have pinned up photographs, torn from pulp-paper magazines, of the "saint of the gutters," Mother Teresa.

Constitution

OF THE INTERNATIONAL ASSOCIATION OF
CO-WORKERS OF MOTHER TERESA
AFFILIATED TO THE MISSIONARIES
OF CHARITY

1. "The International Association of Co-Workers of Mother Teresa" consists of men, women, young people and children of all religions and denominations throughout the world, who seek to love God in their fellow men, through whole hearted free service to the poorest of the poor of all castes and creeds, and who wish to unite themselves in a spirit of prayer and sacrifice with the work of Mother Teresa and the Missionaries of Charity.

2. Mother Teresa's desire is that all Co-Workers, Sisters and Brothers, and the poor unite themselves to each other in prayer and sacrifice:

A. By helping people recognize God in the person of the poor.

B. By helping people love God better through works of charity and service to the poor.

C. By uniting the Missionaries of Charity and Co-Workers throughout the world in prayer and sacrifice.

D. By keeping the family spirit.

E. By fostering aid between various countries and by eliminating duplication of effort and aid for individual centres of the Missionaries of Charity.

3. By "the poor" is meant those who do not have enough to eat, whose living conditions are incompatible with the dignity of the human person, and who are seriously deprived, materially, spiritually or socially, in relation to their neighbors. While hearing the cries of the poor, the Co-Workers will have a special concern for those who are unwanted and unloved.

4. All Co-Workers express their love of God through service to the poor, as Jesus Christ himself has said:

"Whatever you did to the least of these my brethren,
you did it to Me" (Matthew 25: 40).

"For I was hungry, and you gave Me to eat;
I was thirsty, and you gave Me to drink;

I was homeless, and you took Me in;
naked and you clothed Me;
sick and you visited Me;
in prison and you came to see Me" (Matthew 25:35).

5. While remaining sensitive and responsive to the needs of the poor who are near to them, the Co-Workers of Mother Teresa give their support to Mother Teresa and to her Missionaries of Charity in their Mission of love to the poorest of the poor wherever they are found, and thus share in the "whole hearted free service to the poor" which the Sisters and Brothers vow to God.

6. They recognize the dignity, the individuality and the infinite value of every human life.

7. The keynote of the giving is Love and Service.

8. The Co-Workers of Mother Teresa recognize that all the goods of this world—including gifts of mind and body, advantages of birth and education—are the free gifts of God, and that no one has a right to a superfluity of wealth while others are dying of starvation, and suffering from every kind of want. They seek to right this grave injustice by the exercise of voluntary poverty and the sacrifices of luxuries in their way of life.

9. At the same time and in the same spirit, Co-Workers of Mother Teresa make available to the Missionaries of Charity whatever time and material help are within their power to provide.

10. Co-Workers of Mother Teresa unite in prayer with the Missionaries of Charity by saying the following prayer daily:

Make us worthy, Lord, to serve our fellow men throughout the world who live and die in poverty and hunger. Give them, through our hands, this day their daily bread, and by our understanding love give Peace and Joy.

Lord, make me a channel of Thy peace, that where there is hatred I may bring love; that where there is wrong, I may bring the spirit of forgiveness; that where there is discord, I may bring harmony; that where there is error, I may bring truth; that where there is doubt, I may bring faith; that where there is despair, I may bring hope; that where there are shadows, I may bring light; that where there is sadness, I may bring joy.

Lord, grant that I may seek rather to comfort than to be com-

forted; to understand than to be understood; to love than to be loved; for it is by forgetting self that one finds; it is by dying that one awakens to eternal life. Amen.

11.   Co-Workers should emulate the spirit of poverty and humility of the Missionaries of Charity and should avoid unnecessary expenses at their meetings and should conduct all their business affairs with economy and austerity.

12.   As the Missionaries of Charity give whole hearted free service to the poor, so the Co-Workers also and all those in office will give their whole hearted free service.

13.   In accordance with Mother Teresa's wish Co-Workers throughout the world should maintain contact with one another and exchange ideas and information through the INTERNATIONAL COMMITTEE:

PRESIDENT

Mother M. Teresa M.C. (Foundress)

PERMANENT SECRETARY

Sister M. Frederick M.C.
(Missionaries of Charity, 54 A Lower Circular Road,
Calcutta 16, India)

CHAIRMAN

Mrs. Ann Blaikie
(2 Silvermere, Byfleet Road, Cobham, Surrey, England)

VICE-CHAIRMEN

(one per country appointed by Governing Body)

LINK SICK AND SUFFERING CO-WORKERS

Mlle. Jacqueline de Decker
(Rue Prince Albert, Antwerp, Belgium)

14.   GOVERNING BODY According to circumstance and need the President, Chairman and Permanent Secretary and their successors in office shall be the Governing Body, and may omit and amend and add to the rules of the Constitution of "The International Association of Co-Workers of Mother Teresa." No change of aim or constitution may be made by any one else in any country. All officers are voluntary.

15.   YEARLY NEWS BULLETIN

(a) Vice-Chairmen will send to the Chairman by a stated date a short summary of projects undertaken and aid given by their country during the previous year, for inclusion in the Annual Bulletin. Activities undertaken by children should be mentioned separately.

(b) The Bulletin will contain:
(i) News of the Missionaries of Charity.
(ii) Summaries as in (a) above.
(iii) Obituaries among the Co-Workers, Sisters and Brothers (these should be sent to the Chairman as they occur).
(iv) Addresses of the Vice-Chairmen.
(v) Any other matters.

(c) The Vice-Chairmen will be responsible for getting copies made in their own countries and for the distribution of the same.

16.   PRAYER CARDS All are asked to use the prayer cards and to meditate on one chosen passage for a few minutes before the meetings.

17.   DAY OF PRAYER A Day of Prayer and Thanksgiving will be help on the 7th October, throughout the world, being the day on which the Society of the Missionaries of Charity was founded in 1950. On that day all are asked to unite with the Sisters and Brothers in giving thanks to God.

18.   BRANCHES OF THE ASSOCIATION Branches of the Association are established in a number of countries. Normally Co-Workers share in Mother Teresa's work through membership of a small group or as an individual.

19.   SICK AND SUFFERING CO-WORKERS The sick and those unable to join in activities may become a close Co-Worker of an individual Sister or Brother by offering their prayer and suffering for such Sister or Brother.

20.   SEAL The Missionaries of Charity seal will be used only on official correspondence.

ACKNOWLEDGMENTS

The author and the publisher wish to express special thanks to all those members of the Missionaries of Charity who kindly provided information and photographs concerning their work all over the world; and to the following individuals: Lazar Bojaxhiu; Eugen Vogt of the Swiss Co-Workers of Mother Teresa; Malcolm Muggeridge; the editors of *India Today* and the *Yugoslavia Review;* Desmond Doig; and all other persons without whose cooperation this book would not have been completed.

PICTURE CREDITS

Associated Press, Frankfurt: 3, 44 left,
    88 top and center right

Baldev/Sygma, Paris: 72 above left, 74 left,
    75, 77

Basak/Gamma, Paris: 41, 82/83, 87

Bojaxhiu, Lazar, Archives, Palermo: 5,
    24 left, 24 right (Photo: Geir Bølstad),
    25, 27, 74 top, 91 top left (Photo:
    Arne Iversen)

Cambridge Evening News: 101

Comet-Photo, Zurich: 62 top

Eidsoren, Sigurd, Oslo: 11 left

Fincher, Terry, London: 49 top, 50 right

Foto-Present, Essen: 46 left, 49 right, 65, 67,
    72 above right, 73 right, 88 left

Francolon/Gamma, Paris: 12, 48 top, 51 top
    and center, 80/81

Fryda, Dr. Bill, Rochester: 69 right

Gähwyler, Karl, Lucerne: 54 bottom,
    55 bottom, 64

Keystone-Press: 11 right, 89 bottom,
    90 center, 95, 96 top, 99, 104, 107, 108, 115

KNA-Bild, Frankfurt: 8, 28, 29, 38/39,
    42 left, 45, 46/47, 48 left, 50 left,
    51 bottom, 61 bottom, 62 bottom right,
    68 center right, 69 left, 72 above center
    and bottom, 73 left and center, 79, 86,
    91 bottom, 96 left, 97, 102 bottom, 117

Laffont/Sygma, Paris: 56/57

Laurizen, G., Hellerup: 92/93

Pabel, Hilmar, Umratshausen am Chiemsee:
    6, 52/53, 89 above

Paris-Match: 109, 110/111, 113

Peter, Günter, Berlin: 90 top

Publisher's Archives: 20, 98,
    103 center and right

Rai, Raghu/Magnum, Paris: 42 bottom,
    48 bottom, 58/59, 60 right, 119, 120/121

Reist, Dölf, Interlaken: 32/33

Ringier Bilderdienst, Zurich: 71, 100 top,
    103 top and left

Scala, Florence: 13

Schneiders, Toni, Lindau/B: 16 right

Sipa-Press, Paris: 9, 105, 112

Smurfit Publications, Dublin: 30, 31

Süddeutscher Verlag, Munich: 16 left,
    102 top

Staffelbach, Franz, Büren: 49 bottom, 68 top

Teki, New Delhi: 37, 44 bottom

Vogt, Eugen, Archives Swiss Branch of
    International Co-Workers of Mother
    Teresa, Lucerne: 33 right, 34, 35, 42 top,
    43, 44 top (PH: Karl Gähwyler), 54 left
    (PH: Dr. Ola Lundin), 54/55 (PH:
    Dr. A. Chlapowski), 55 center, 60 left
    (PH: Theo van Boogaard), 61 top
    (PH: F. Kämper), 61 center, 62 left
    (PH: Dr. Chlapowski), 63 (PH: Missio-
    Munich), 100 center left (FAO Rome)

Yugoslav Review, Belgrade: 2, 14/15
    (Photo: B. Budimovski), 18, 19 top,
    bottom left and bottom right (Photo:
    B. Budimovski), 19 bottom center
    (Photo: P. Popesku), 21, 22/23, 36

INDEX